M6/201756

BJ 1725 B4
C. 1
BENSMAN, JOSEPH.
DOLLARS AND SENSE : IDEOLOGY,

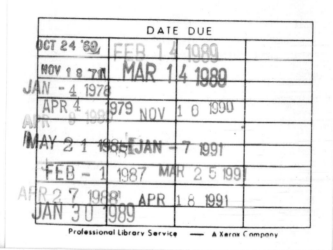

DATE DUE			
OCT 24 '69	FEB 1 4 1980		
NOV 1 8 70	MAR 1 4 1980		
JAN - 4 1976			
APR 4 1979	NOV 1 0 1990		
APR 9 1997			
MAY 2 1 1986	JAN - 7 1991		
FEB - 1 1987	MAR 2 5 1991		
APR 2 7 1988	APR 1 8 1991		
JAN 3 0 1989			

Professional Library Service —— A Xerox Company

DOLLARS *and* SENSE

By the same author
Small Town and Mass Society *(with A. J. Vidich)*
Mass, Class and Bureaucracy *(with Bernard Rosenberg)*
Reflections on the Community *(with A. J. Vidich and M. Stein)*

JOSEPH BENSMAN

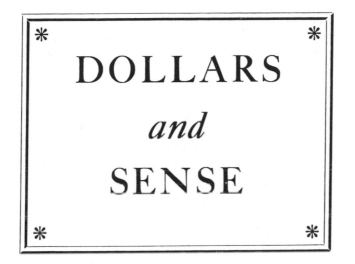

DOLLARS
and
SENSE

*Ideology, Ethics, and the Meaning of Work
in Profit and Nonprofit Organizations*

THE MACMILLAN COMPANY, NEW YORK

COLLIER-MACMILLAN LTD., LONDON

Copyright © 1967 by Joseph Bensman

All rights reserved. No part of this book may be reproduced or transmitted in any form or by any means, electronic or mechanical, including photocopying, recording or by any information storage and retrieval system, without permission in writing from the Publisher.

Library of Congress Catalog Card Number: 67-13586

First Printing

The Macmillan Company, New York
Collier-Macmillan Canada Ltd., Toronto, Ontario
Printed in the United States of America

Acknowledgment is made to Peter L. Berger, who kindly permitted reprint of "The Advertising Man," written by Joseph Bensman under the pseudonym of Ian Lewis, from *The Human Shape of Work,* edited by Petèr L. Berger and published by The Macmillan Company, copyright © 1964 by Peter L. Berger.

To:
DAVID, RHEA, *and* MIRIAM

CONTENTS

DOLLARS *and* SENSE

INTRODUCTION

ALTHOUGH THEY REFLECT a lifelong interest, the studies in this volume, on the meaning of work and work ethics, have a purely accidental origin. The study of advertising came into being because Peter Berger, who was editing a book on ethics and the meaning of work, asked me to write an essay on the subject which later appeared in his book *The Human Shape of Work*. Berger knew of my interest in the subject, and had previously read and heard of a number of articles and talks I had written or given on it.

At the time he asked me to do the essay, I had been working for over eight years as a consumer research manager in one of the larger New York advertising agencies. During that time I had been informally and compulsively conducting a participant observation study and had been interviewing (surreptitiously) a large number of officials in my own and other agencies. The word "surreptitiously" is used advisedly. All such interviews were conducted without the respondent's knowing that he was being interviewed, and all were conducted on an informal basis, so that no respondent could act in the official "role" of respondent. As a result, I feel that I received little cant or "public relations" responses in these interviews. Moreover, in most cases I was able to observe the behavior of the respondent as well as record his verbal responses. I could see him as he stepped out of his public and official role, into a personal and private role in which he could thus comment on his own public behavior and describe the social, psychological, or economic "realities" that governed it.

In part this opportunity came about only because I was able to establish a personal "unofficial" relationship with the

individuals whom we can now pompously label as "respondents." This relationship was based upon a trust (1) that I was
not doing a study and (2) that I would not gossip to the
respondent's peers, bosses, or clients. While I was in the
agency, I maintained, so far as I know, the latter part of that
trust. The write-up of the essay was so done, I hope, that
individuals per se were not recognizable. To put it differently,
I hoped that my descriptions applied to so many people that
each person could feel that they applied to someone else, and
no one could feel that they applied to himself.

Since the original publication of the essay, I have checked
back with many of the people I interviewed and found that
these hopes were fulfilled. No one felt insulted, and all felt
that they could recognize a portrait of someone else in the
study.

As a matter of record, all respondents who had read the
study and with whom I talked after the study felt that I had,
on the whole, presented an accurate and sympathetic picture
of the advertising agency; and most felt I had done a necessary job of explaining to the lay public "what it really is like."
The one exception, the editor of an advertising trade paper,
felt that my data were inaccurate, that I was doing a smear of
advertising, and that I was so biased that he could not finish
the essay. One other person, it was reported to me, felt that
the study was not objective.

Most of my friends who were not in advertising felt that I
was doing an exposé of the "money-grabbing hucksters" and
felt vindicated by that exposé in selecting less profitable and
more noble occupations. Since this was not my conscious
purpose, I felt that the essay had failed in that respect. In
part, the essays on ethics and meaning of work in nonprofit
organizations address themselves to this issue.

Needless to say, writing these essays on advertising and on
nonprofit organizations is an unethical act. In a sense it is an
act of disloyalty to those who employed me, those whom I
interviewed, and the clients of the agency in which I worked.
I was aware of this at the time I did the essay for the Berger
book, and I tried to prevent any harmful effects to myself and
to others by using a pseudonym and substantive and stylistic

devices which disguised the organization and personnel involved. I described a hypothetical advertising agency rather than a specific one, and I used as examples incidents which could have occurred and did occur in a large number of agencies. In these instances I sacrificed verisimilitude for ease of conscience. I don't think I altered any essential fact or conclusion. In republishing this essay under my own name, I now compound that ethical lapse. In writing on social work, poverty programs, and "the university," I continue to be unethical. In each of these areas I have directly observed many of the personnel in question. I have interviewed them without, in most cases, letting them know that they were being interviewed. In the studies of the university and social work, I have synthetically described a vast number of institutions, making no special reference to any one. In the study of the Community Action Program, I have presented a synthetic history of one agency. Insiders may well recognize the agency, although some particulars relative to individuals in that agency are altered. In no case have I knowingly altered any facts which would affect my interpretation or conclusions. However, I may well be wrong in drawing this final conclusion.

These "ethical lapses" reflect an inevitable conflict in ethics in the social sciences. Most research conducted by social scientists is done on distant populations, criminals, delinquents, Negroes and other minority groups, industrial workers and members of "primitive" societies. Because the population is distant (socially or geographically) it is possible to do honest work. When the social scientist does work in his own backyard, the work is most frequently highly technical, bland, and/or fraudulent. This is only to say that the social scientist must protect himself and his immediate social world from the consequences of those exposures which are taken for granted when studying a distant population. As a result most social research central to the institutional problems of middle- and upper-class life and institutions usually is not very accurate.

To solve this problem I would make a modest proposal: Every social scientist should have a pseudonym. The pseudonym would be used to sign articles that the writer thinks might be embarrassing to his organization if he writes them in his public role as representative and symbol of that organization. The real name of the author could be an open secret between author and his respondents. By pretending that the pseudonymous author was a real, but unknown person, all parties would be protected from the consequences of exposure; and, as a result, the author, under the cover of the pseudonym, could attempt to describe what they thought was the reality he was observing.

In effect this is what happened with respect to "In the Courts of Power." It caused no scandal, because a great number of relevant individuals were unaware of the existence of the study, and those who were aware of it, felt that no one else was. As a result all readers could respond to the essay in their roles as private individuals and ignore it publicly.

One of the consequences, perhaps the most important one for me, of doing the essay on advertising, was a voluntary decision to leave advertising for the "nobler" and more disinterested research in the university and in a number of other nonprofit agencies.

When the essay "In the Courts of Power" appeared it was favorably reviewed in a number of journals. At that time, another consequence of use of a pseudonym became apparent. Since I had received recognition for the essay only through the use of the pseudonym, I began to hate Ian Lewis (my pseudonym) for denying recognition to Joseph Bensman. When Clement Alexandre, my publisher, suggested I expand my original essay or write additional ones, I felt I could not resist the temptation to expose Ian Lewis and to claim credit for my work. Since I have been out of advertising for more than two years, I feel that there is little reason for not doing so.

Since leaving the advertising business, I have been employed in more dignified work. I have been a Professor of Sociology at the City University of New York and have been engaged as a consultant and research director of several antipoverty programs. Prior to my flight from Madison Avenue, I had worked as a college professor on both a part- and a full-time basis and as an employee and consultant to a number of public and private nonprofit agencies. I had also done studies of ethics and the meaning of work in several of these agencies. My essays on nonprofit work reflect my experience in these areas.

This experience also has served as an opportunity to contrast and compare the profit and nonprofit agencies, as reported in these essays. The essays on the university in particular may provide a basis for evaluating my decision to leave advertising in favor of academia.

Since much of Part III of this work deals with plagiarism and the ethics of borrowing and acknowledging ideas, it is incumbent upon me (at least in this work) to acknowledge my sources. I am indebted to Israel Gerver, Bernard Rosenberg, and Arthur J. Vidich for much more than I can consciously account. In doing collaborative work with them it has been difficult for me to sort out my own contributions and theirs. This work undoubtedly reflects ideas that emerged in such collaborations.

In a deeper sense I am indebted to H. H. Gerth, who, as a teacher and friend, provided me many of the basic ideas that animate this and much of my other research and writing. My early study with Selig Perlman at the University of Wisconsin also has influenced my subsequent work, much more perhaps than I am fully aware. For as I think about my own "original contributions" I increasingly and disturbingly find ideas enunciated by Perlman at the core.

In the same way, I feel that much of my work reflects a persistent interest in the works of Max Weber, Freud, Karl Mannheim, Marx, and Veblen. Needless to say, I will be forced to bear the responsibility for my own interpretations and misinterpretation of these thinkers.

In writing these essays I have attempted to rely upon my own direct observations and interviews of persons in the relevant work areas. In doing so, I have avoided reading and rereading other works that might force me to substitute secondary interpretations for my own. I cannot be unaware, however, that my own response to other works in this area might have influenced my own observation and interpretation. These include Mills' *Sociological Imagination,* Caplow and McGee's *Academic Marketplace,* Carr-Saunders' *Professions,* and Laski's *American Democracy.*

I would like to acknowledge the contributions of a number of my students who submitted research reports and personal observations on their work experience. In doing so, they enabled me to check my own observations, in order to satisfy me that they were not the unique conjurings of a bizarre imagination. On the basis of these checks, I have, at least, been able to feel that these observations are social in character; they have that much objectivity. For the rest, the reader must and will make his own judgments. The students are Moon Eng, Michael Givant, Sylvan Felstein, Jerry Levy, Tom Shey, and Beverly Bert.

Henry Surval provided many of the detailed statistical data and much of the research on the economics of the advertising agency. Bernhard Greenblatt, Israel Gerver, and Joseph Lagey, Gloria and Irving Dlugacz, and Jack Yampolsky provided me with valuable information concerning aspects of their work settings which was not directly accessible to my observation.

Finally I would like to thank Wally Osterholz for her devoted work in typing the manuscript.

Yet, after all these acknowledgments are made, both the virtues and vices of this and any other work ultimately are the products of the author.

PART I

*

*The Advertising Man
and His Work,
Its Organization, Ethics,
and Meaning*

THE ADVERTISING MAN

ADVERTISING, MORE than any other institution in contemporary society, is a cynosure. It symbolizes and concentrates in its image all that is considered both good and bad in present-day commercial and industrial capitalism in America. The importance attached to advertising by laymen, by businessmen, and by advertising men themselves far outweighs its numerical importance. Only 65,000 people are directly employed in advertising agencies in this country, a small number compared with, let us say, the number of doctors (230,000), public school teachers (1.5 million), or plumbers (333,000).

Nevertheless, advertising men do have important economic functions. In 1965 about $15.3 billion was spent on advertising. This money was actually spent by American businessmen, not by advertising-agency executives. Advertising men at the most consulted, recommended, and advised businessmen on this expenditure. Only a small part was directly spent by advertising men in the preparation of print advertisements, TV and radio commercials, car cards (advertisements on buses, subways, trains, and trucks), and billboards. For advising on the total expenditure and for preparing these advertisements, advertising agencies received commissions that are approximately 15 percent of the total outlay by the clients. Thus the net commissions of advertising agencies are approximately $1 billion, 100 million, which, compared with the size of the gross operating income of the automotive industry ($12 billion, 700 million*) or of the steel industry ($8 billion, 400 million), can be described only as small potatoes.

* Value added to the cost of raw materials.

Yet advertising as an industry is as much a cynosure for American society as is the automobile industry or the steel industry. This is because these are basic industries (with some exception taken to amount of waste in the design and the annual turnover of automobile models), while advertising is a controversial issue and institution in American society.

At the simplest levels, academic, aesthetic, intellectual, and cultural leaders continually attack advertising for being the source of all of the moral, cultural, and intellectual depravity and bad taste in American mass media. Such an attack overstates the cases because, in the first instance, advertising men only recommend the shows, programs, and placements of advertising to their clients. The final responsibility rests with the client, but when criticism is made, advertising men are the public scapegoat. They are paid to be so, and many wish that they had the actual influence or power that the critics attribute to them. Advertising is charged with stressing only the material, sexual, and vulgar lower values in the human personality. It is charged with stimulating the sense of individual inadequacy by reminding individuals of their imperfections and their unattained goals, and in raising hopes for the achievement of unattainable goals.

At a more sinister level, advertising men are attributed the powers of a Svengali, the sinister *deus ex machina,* who by devious and highly developed psychological, linguistic, and artistic devices brainwashes the American public. It is charged with controlling the foci of the public's attention, feeding the public lies, and operating on its unconscious and irrational faculties so that people cannot make rational decisions. In fact, the most serious charge made against advertising is that it destroys the capacity for rational behavior, makes men infants, and by creating these habits of thought destroys the psychological and intellectual capacity for democratic decision-making and for self-government.

As compared with the severity of this charge, direct or indirect charges aimed at the media-selection functions of advertising appear to be secondary. Advertising men, insofar as they are advisers for their clients, are charged with bringing about the demise of numerous magazines and of weakening the strength of independent newspapers and radio as media, simply because their impersonal concern (correctly or incorrectly assessed) for economic efficiency has resulted in the shift of much agency advertising money (34 percent) to television. Whether advertising agencies had the power to make these decisions, or whether the decisions made were simply objective recognition of inescapable facts, is for the moment beside the point. What is central is the fact that advertising is the object of scorn and criticism for possessing in a high degree precisely those characteristics for which our entire society is criticized.

In a peculiar way, however, advertising men are romanticized and envied for possessing the same characteristics that are criticized. They are seen as supermen or superidiots who live in Ivy League or "gray flannel" suits. They are pictured as leading glamorous lives over expensive lunches, entertaining either fatuous or overdemanding clients, and indulging in sexual promiscuity for business reasons or as an escape from the frustrations of business. They are described as leading barren but exciting lives in suburbs or exurbs, with alcohol and their own and other people's wives, neglecting their children and, by ill-thought-out political gestures, upsetting the politics of their sterile but expensive communities.

Advertising men are articulate and do not take their criticism in silence. They add to the controversy by attacking the long-haired, irresponsible, negativistic, brainless professors, aesthetes, and faggots who never met a payroll and who would undermine the American way of life out of envy of the success of their superiors.

They answer the specific charges by "proving" that advertising provides an essential function for an ever-expanding American economy by stimulating new needs and new wants, which only an expanding industry can satisfy. It accelerates the process of "creative destruction" which, in Schumpeter's terms, provides capitalism with its dynamism and growth.

Advertising, it is asserted, creates markets for new products and expands the markets for old ones. It forces the research and development departments of major manufacturers to experiment continually and to achieve scientific miracles that enable one competitor to raise the quality of its brand over that of another. For advertising, the argument goes, is the soul of competition, and competition is the heart of American enterprise and its free enterprise economy.

On the cultural front, advertising via the mass media is allegedly an important vehicle for the dissemination of serious culture and political awareness. Advertisers support, when it is economically feasible, the production of Shakespeare on radio and television, the ballet, the symphony, and the opera on television, together with news programs, documentaries, and "specials." Moreover, advertisers support newspapers and serious magazines, as well as entertainment in magazines. And, finally, they make it possible, it is reasoned, for newspapers to educate and inform the American public.

Advertising per se informs the public, the argument continues, of the range of brands available, provides information as to the virtues of these brands ("You can't expect advertisers to knock their own products"), and makes it easy for individuals to make "consumer choices."

We expect the controversy to continue indefinitely, to wax and wane, as journalists, moralists, politicians, and intellectuals mount new attacks and are repulsed, or when the issues die for a time because of the exhaustion of the protagonists and of a weary public to whom all of the words are too familiar.

The controversy over advertising and advertising men will probably never be resolved at the ideological level. Nor can advertising be understood at that level. Advertising is an industry, composed of separate firms, agencies, each of which has a highly organized internal structure and distinctive but not uniform methods of dealing with its separate clientele, subsidiary organizations (media agencies and subcontractors), the government, and the public. Surrounding the individual agencies are associations of advertising agencies (the "four A's"—Association of Advertising Agencies of America —the Advertising Council, and professional associations composed of the respective technical and professional specialists, employees of a wide variety of agencies). To complete our schematic outline, there are personal and informal cliques that make up a series of interlocking friendship and acquaintance patterns that cut across agency lines, departmental lines, and in some cases, client, agency, and subcontractor lines of communication.

In all the above formal respects, the advertising business does not differ from other businesses. Our discussion will therefore be confined to those aspects of the advertising business that are either unique or that are accentuated much more than is usual in other businesses. We shall, therefore, describe the structure of the advertising industry in order to set the stage for a more detailed discussion of advertising as a drama in which some of the ethical and moral dilemmas at work in our society are acted out.

ECONOMIC AND STRUCTURAL CHARACTERISTICS OF THE ADVERTISING AGENCY

1. ADVERTISING is a labor-intensive and capital-extensive industry. The advertising agency makes no great investments in capital goods. Its major capital investments are in typewriters, calculating machines (and in a few large agencies the rental of computers), duplicating equipment, and office furniture. The rental of office space is the major fixed cost of an agency. By and large, labor costs—primarily salaries—are the single largest item in agency costs. Labor costs on an average constitute 70 percent of the annual operating costs of an advertising agency.

Because of the absence of an elaborate machine technology and the corresponding presence of labor-intensivity, advertising is properly called a service industry. Advertising men emphasize this service feature of the agency until the truth becomes a cliché. The composite cliché is as follows: "All we have to offer our clients is a service—our skill, our knowl-

edge, our brains, our talent, our know-how, and our judgment. All we create are ideas, plans, slogans, and arrangements of words, pictures, sounds, and symbols. To the extent
that we execute these functions well, and only to the extent
that our clients have need for these functions, are we entitled
to the high fees, commissions, and salaries we earn."

If an agency can succeed in convincing a prospective client
that these claims are true (and they are claims until proved or
disproved by subsequent actions), the agency can make a
powerful case. For American business has a continuous need
for "brains," ideas, judgment, wisdom, counsel, and know-
how. It is by now a truism that most major brands of consumer goods are not distinguishable from one another to the
consumer when he tests them by means of blind-product
tests. If this is true, the tremendous differences in the sales
success of various competitive brands are primarily due to
differences in the marketing effectiveness of the competitive
manufacturers, including advertising.

In a number of industries the marketing organizations of
the manufacturers (the sales and distribution organizations,
the financial reserves, the dealer-relations programs, merchandising and sales-promotion programs) are considered to
be at a parity. However, some companies have made tremendous sales successes with the introduction of new brands
and the revitalizing of declining brands, while the equally
well-marketed competitive brands (aside from advertising)
have suffered declines or only moderate gains in sales.

Thus slogans like "Winston tastes good like a cigarette
should" or "Be sociable, have a Pepsi" have been worth hundreds of millions of dollars to their respective manufacturing
companies.

However, since the advertising agencies' claim for their
value to business is based on the intangibles of skill, talent,
knowledge, know-how, and so on, and not on objective technological processes, the client can at any time reject the
claim, especially since every advertising agency makes substantially the same claim in attempting to seduce accounts
from other agencies.

2. While we have stressed the fact that the operating in-

come of agencies is relatively small, the number of persons engaged in advertising is still smaller. The labor-intensity of advertising thus consists of a relatively small number of highly paid specialized technicians and managerial officials.

A large-sized but not gigantic agency with billings of approximately $100 million will have an operating income of $15 million. If we allow all costs but labor costs and profits not to exceed $3.5 million, then direct and indirect payments to personnel will amount to $11.5 million. Such an agency, if well run, may employ from six hundred to seven hundred people. The average agency income available for profits and payments to personnel is thus in the neighborhood of $16,000 to $18,000 per employee. Since at least 60 percent of the employees of an advertising agency are relatively low-paid clerical, bookkeeping, and stenographic help, the average amount of money available for the professional, creative, and managerial staff is estimated at (depending upon whether the agency employs six hundred or seven hundred persons in total) from $27,000 to $34,000 per professional employee. Since many agencies are owned by their professional, creative, and managerial staffs, salaries, profits, and profit-sharing funds can at times be considered as part of the same pool.

Of course, not all agencies are so profitable as our hypothetical but not improbable agency. And, of course, we have been dealing with averages—averages in salaries and an equal distribution in stock throughout the professional staff. Both of these assumptions are contrary to fact. There is great range in the salary levels of various professional, creative, and managerial officials of an agency. And even while many agencies are "employee-owned," the chief officers and executives are likely to own the lion's share of stock, with middle- and lower-level officials owning just enough to satisfy the Bureau of Internal Revenue (that the company is employee-owned and not a proprietorship) and the implicit or explicit demands of these lower-ranking officials for equity. These latter demands are granted either to keep valued employees happy or to seduce them from a competitive agency.

The following table indicates average salary range of a number of typical positions in a relatively large advertising agency,

according to the director of the largest employment agency
servicing the advertising business:

Account Supervisor	$30,000–$40,000
Account Executive	$15,000–$25,000
Asst. Account Executive	$ 6,000–$12,000
Merchandising Director	$25,000–$35,000
Asst. Merchandising Director	$15,000–$20,000
Market Research Director	$20,000–$40,000
Media Director	$20,000–$40,000
Media Buyer	$10,000–$15,000
Junior Media Buyer	$ 5,200–$ 6,500
Creative Director	$25,000–$60,000
Copy Chief	$35,000–$45,000
Copy Supervisor	$25,000–$35,000
Copy Group Head	$18,000–$30,000
Copywriter	$ 8,000–$18,000
Head Art Director	$30,000–$45,000
Group Head Art Director	$20,000–$25,000
Art Director	$12,000–$20,000
Art Director (Board)	$10,000–$15,000
TV Art Director	$15,000–$25,000
TV Story Board Artist	$ 8,000–$12,000
Production Manager	$12,000–$18,000

Salaries, per se, cover only part of the perquisites of the
advertising man. Profit-sharing plans allow the agency official
to accumulate a retirement fund or a separation allowance
that may result in a yearly deferred income of up to 20
percent of his annual income, which when collected is taxable
at capital-gains rates.

Stock options and increases in the value of stock in the
agency (whose prices are artificially pegged by the company)
provide additional capital gains. The opportunity to acquire
stock, however, is more than a capital gain, a way of evading
taxes when one moves up the income ladder. Stock acquisition is a genuine method of becoming wealthy, based on
talent alone, as the agency defines talent. Since the advertising agency is a capital-extensive and labor-intensive industry,

the physical assets of an agency do not constitute a limit to stock acquisition. One does not "water" the stock (physical assets) by issuing more stock (equity shares), since the physical assets are of little value in themselves. The issuance of stock to an individual simply means that his "services" represent an important part of the service that the agency sells to its actual or prospective clients. Of course, if an individual makes known to his bosses his estimate of his own worth, they are more likely to calculate the value of that individual's services in terms of the total matrix of the agency's total income-earning services, and reward him accordingly.

All of this means that valued individuals can easily acquire stock, and can do so at a very young age. Stock acquisition is made easy by issuance of new low-price issues, by options, and by deferred-payment plans. The ease of stock acquisition means that in advertising, the American dream of rags-to-riches can be realized in a sufficient number of cases to serve as goad and pull to thousands of young men in advertising who may be on the make.

That the agency president and majority stockholder of a $100 million (billing) corporation is the son of Italian immigrants, or that another may be the son of a Jewish rag buyer, is both a reality and a myth. The reality is one that can be illustrated by thousands of examples, and everyone in the advertising business has his own favorite illustration. The use of this reality becomes the myth for these thousands of others, and enables them to sustain the pace that advertising demands of them.

The countermyth that advertising opportunities are reserved for "bright" young men from Ivy League schools is also true, but less true. Bright young men from Ivy League schools are especially valued to the extent that their lack of enough imagination to know the difficulties inherent in their work enables them to act with poise, confidence, and with sufficiently good manners to charm and gain the confidence of clients. Such charm, poise, self-confidence, and manners are as important as skill and talent in gaining and retaining clients.

Despite all this, the agency approach to rewarding its personnel is to reward those whom it must (nothing is given away) for whatever talents appear to be necessary. Thus Ivy Leaguers and non-Ivy Leaguers, Catholics and Jews, are rewarded. Since a wide variety of types of ability can be used to justify an agency, a wide variety of talents is rewarded. On the whole, this works in favor of the able, regardless of origin.

Becoming a millionaire is thus the major promise that the myth of advertising offers to the able. It is not the only promise. To those who know they will be moderately successful but will not become wealthy the opportunity to live as if one were rich is almost as seductive. This is done through "fringe benefits."

Advertising men are the customers of the media representatives (television and radio networks and stations, newspapers, magazines, and outdoor advertising), of television and commercials production companies, of graphic-arts firms, of research firms, and of thousands of would-be suppliers of services. The standard way of selling one's services is to wine and dine the agency representative who is reputed to have even a minor voice in a "buying decision." Thus an agency official (in New York) with an $8,000-a-year salary, or more, will be wined and dined at one of the hundreds of "expense accounts" restaurants or hotels. He will eat and drink at the Plaza, the Waldorf-Astoria, the Commodore, the New Yorker, the "21" Club, or Crist Sella's. If he is deemed really important, he then receives the supreme accolade by dining at the Chauveron, the Four Seasons, or the Forum of the Twelve Caesars. The ubiquity of the free lunch reflects the lack of centralization in advertising. Almost anyone can influence the buying decision. In manufacturing, purchasing is centralized.

At the same time that he is being wined and dined, the agency official may read magazines that come by free subscription, drink whiskey that is part of his Christmas loot, or present his children with toys that are given to him as promotion pieces to advertise a product. If the agency man is truly unscrupulous, and if he has or can convince a prospective supplier that he has great buying power, the gift he receives may be a car, a boat, a European vacation, or sexual access to starlets, models, or television beauties. The public image of the advertising man is not entirely wrong.

The other side of the wining-and-dining complex is almost equally attractive (if one is attracted). The agency man is the supplier for the advertiser or the client. As such, his job is to wine and dine the client. Everything that advertisers do for the agency man can be and is done for the client. There are some differences, however. The amount spent on entertainment is expected to be appropriate both to the position of the agency man and to the position of the entertainee in the client organization. One is not expected to take a "clerk" to the Chauveron, nor is a "clerk" expected to entertain the president or the advertising manager of the client firm. If he does, he appears to be arrogating the position of his bosses.

There are other differences. When entertained by the suppliers, a low-level agency official can be gay, carefree, and expansive, even to a high-ranking official in the supplier firm. When he entertains the client, a high-ranking agency man must, if necessary, pretend deference even to a low-ranking official in the client firm. Thus mobility in temperament becomes a role requirement for the advertising man.

The expense account thus becomes a major way for a man of modest income to live, during the day, as if he were rich. And this quality of life is far more important psychologically than any increment in income the agency man can gain by cheating on the expense account.

There is some prestige attached by one's peers to having a legitimate reason for eating "for free" frequently; and peers will "keep score" on the size of the tab and the number of times one does so. For agency men accept the myth of the glamour of advertising as much as does the lay public. The poignancy of this acceptance is illustrated at the time when the luncheon appointment is canceled at the last moment and the agency man finds himself eating hamburgers at Nedick's instead of *pâté de foie gras* at the Chauveron. (No discussion will take place here on the response of the wife who, after preparing a fancy dinner, discovers that her husband is not hungry because he has had a three-hour lunch at the Chauveron.)

We have described the favorable economic and romantic myths and realities surrounding advertising that spring essentially from its labor-intensity. The economic disadvantages also spring from this labor-intensity. Whenever an agency loses an account, or whenever it is deemed necessary to cut operating expenses, the largest single pool of expenses is the pool available for salaries and wages (since over two-thirds of all agency expenses are in this category). Similarly, since the major concentration of labor costs is the high salaries offered to creative, technical, and managerial staffs, the major opportunities for cost-cutting are in this area. To state it differently, firing clerks and secretaries to cut costs is not particularly effective, since the salaries for these categories do not contribute much to costs.

This potential vulnerability of the upper management in the agency business is from time to time made an actuality when accounts shift. The agency that loses a major account (from $2 million to $25 million) finds itself in a cost-income squeeze. If the account lost represents a sizable proportion of its billings, the other accounts cannot bear the burden of maintaining the salaries of the executives. Wholesale firings are likely to ensue. However, since many account personnel work on more than one account, if they are fired because of the loss of one account they are unavailable for work on other accounts. The clients of these other accounts may resent the loss of favored copywriters, account executives, commercial producers, or media planners and take their accounts out of the agency. Thus the loss of one major account may start a vicious cycle that in a number of specific instances has resulted in the sudden demise of large and profitable agencies.

Account shifts in the agency business are fairly frequent. In 1965, 484 accounts shifted, representing $384 million of billings, and approximately $57,600,000 in commissions. The loss of a $2-million account is likely to result in the loss of ten jobs with an average salary of $20,000 (unless these jobs are absorbed by other accounts in the agency losing that account); the loss of a $25-million account is likely to lead to the loss of 188 jobs (assuming the same conditions).

When such losses occur, the job market becomes flooded with applicants, including many inivdiuals who have the same general qualifications. Whether such enforced mobility constitutes an asset or a liability to the career aspirations of an individual depends on the opportunities available at the time of loss of job. In advertising, the loss of job by competent, capable, and blameless men constitutes a major career obstacle.

Theoretically, when an account shifts, just as many new jobs are created as are lost. This is not true in fact, since the agency to which the account shifts will attempt to maximize profits by "doubling up," using hitherto untapped "capital resources" before it employs new people.

Moreover, even if an agency has to "staff up" to absorb a new account, the permanent staff of that agency will view the new acquisition as an opportunity for advancement to new positions, new titles, and salary and stock-acquisition benefits. It is for this reason that the individual who had a good position with the agency losing the account is not likely to be desired by the agency gaining the account. Moreover, since an account shifts because the client is "unhappy" with his former agency, the most visible officials in the losing agency (with some exceptions) are likely to be *persona non grata* to the client and thus to the gaining agency.

Thus it frequently happens that precisely those people who have been most successful in the past, and who appeared to be most worthy of the high salaries they were earning prior to the involuntary loss of job, have the most difficulty relocating. As a result, every individual in advertising knows a person or knows of a person who was "near the top" who has become unemployable through no fault of his own. Such individuals may go into the consulting business, sometimes profitably and sometimes using the fiction that being self-employed justifies the absence of any substantial income. Others retire at a young age and live modestly off the gains from profit-sharing plans and the capital gains from the forced sale of their stock in the company that let them go. Still others become stock and mutual-fund salesmen or real-estate agents, attempting to sell to their former colleagues.

Some, the younger ones, may become schoolteachers—a profession that is continuously enriched by talented, able, but unfortunate victims of the economics of the mass media. A few go into family businesses, if they are fortunate enough to have a family business available. Some relocate at salaries that may range from one-third to one-half their former salaries, and these may recoup their losses if they do not become embittered in the process. Some, especially if their skills are used in the creative departments (art, copywriting, musical composition, and so on), may shift jobs without penalty.

Thus the great opportunities in advertising are offset by the equally great opportunities for total defeat and loss. A job on Madison Avenue appears to be a game of chance, perhaps roulette, or even Russian roulette. In fact, for a time the phrase "Madison Avenue roulette" meant that the last man to lose his nerve was the man who would win. A job on Madison Avenue is a tontine, a last-man's club, where the victims are the living dead, embarrassing reminders that "it could happen to you."

The atmosphere of gambling that characterizes all aspects of the agency business is reinforced by the defenselessness of the agency and its personnel in the face of the whim, fancy, and even perhaps of the wisdom and ability of the client. This ambiguity is the opposite side of the coin from the confidence, assertiveness, and brazenness that advertising men exhibit in making a pitch, when they claim that advertising can do anything and everything.

The ambiguity that represents the greatest opportunity and menace for a specific agency is simply based upon the inability, in all but extreme situations (as previously specified), to measure the value, efficiency, and effectiveness of a specific advertising idea, advertisement, or campaign. Sales may go up fantastically, and sometimes both the agency and client may be in a frenzy to know why. This becomes a problem because, if one does not know what one is doing to make sales go up, any change may be disastrous. Second, if one's gains are thought to be due to chance, then chance can convert the gains to losses just as easily. Similarly, sales losses do occur even after it appears that every step taken by the agency and the client has been thought out carefully, planned, researched, and pretested, and when all concerned have been convinced they have a winner.

The "irrationality" of the marketplace is a source of anxiety, despite the fact that every step may be taken to rule out chance. Research, surveys, pretesting, test markets, controlled experiments—all are attempts to eliminate this ambiguity and irrationality. But the failure to anticipate, to prevent one's "best laid plans" from going astray, is part of the very structure of the market. So many things go into the marketing operation, of which advertising is only a small part, that it is almost impossible to isolate the contribution of a single commercial, slogan, campaign, piece of artwork, or media plan. One can specify all the factors that might conceivably lead to sales success, but one recognizes that each factor applies to one's own brand and one's own marketing operation (including advertising) and also applies to each of a dozen competing brands and to each of a dozen product classes that do not compete directly but do constitute substitute methods of consumer-income disposal. Thus, a brand of beer may compete with all other brands of beer in its sales area (though all brands do not compete uniformly throughout the entire sales areas), with whiskey (by brands and types), with other types of nonessentials, and with, as in the case of shoes, brands and types of necessities.

For each competitive situation, then, there may be several hundred factors that affect the success of the advertised brand. Several thousand factors, therefore, may affect sales success. As if this were not bad enough, it is almost impossible to isolate each factor as it operates in the marketplace. The marketing operation is so complex that each factor is simply one small element in a causal chain, but unusual success or failure in any one factor can affect the total chain.

A further complexity is introduced by the fact that it is extremely difficult to measure each factor separately or to measure two or more factors together in terms of a common

scale of values. In the latter case, it is as difficult to measure
the relative importance of each factor as it is to measure the
factors themselves. Moreover, the factors involved in any
"marketing chain" are continuously changing. Each successful or unsuccessful attempt at measurement may become an-
cient history before the measurement is completed.

All research—marketing, sales, copy, product, package,
consumer, motivational, media, merchandising, test-market,
image, and operations research—represents attempts by the
client or agency to narrow the ambiguity or to reduce the risk
in making decisions. And all these methods must confront the
difficulties of action in a complex "irrational" and uncontrolled market for which there are limited and imprecise
measures. Over $400 million is invested in marketing research
in one year by agencies and by clients in their anxious attempts
to overcome the irrationality of the marketplace.

The feeling of anxiety and powerlessness held by top executives in the face of the tremendous responsibilities placed
upon them for sales and advertising success constitutes the
largest single opportunity for both missionaries and charlatans in the field of advertising research. There is a cycle in
research that begins when a "charismatic" hero discovers a
new approach—the large-scale sample survey, program ana-
lyzing, the store audit, image research, motivation research,
operations research, semantic differential, scales, scaling research, computer simulation, or linear programming, to name
a few. After each such "discovery," there is an intensified
assault on the sales resistance of top agency and client officials to prove conclusively that once the new method is
adopted, rationality and "science" will govern marketing.
Many of the methods and services are "bought," and the new
crusade begins. After the results of such research are in, the
method is either discarded or absorbed as a minor tool in the
inventory of available methods for research. The method,
when absorbed, develops its defenders, who now resist the
claims of new crusaders who possess another final solution.
The failure of such methods to allay the sense of powerlessness and anxiety in the face of an irrational market is attested
by the fact that each new discovery is superseded by a newer
one which, in time, will be superseded.

MAL SPINA COLLEGE LIBRAR

This does not mean that research methods are universally useless. It does mean that, in the light of the complexity of marketing, research works best when there is a clearly defined, specific problem which can be so stated that a specific research finding can, in advance, be interpreted as offering a solution to the problem. Thus small, undignified, and inelegant studies frequently are the most useful, simply because there was a reason for undertaking them. However, these small studies do not have the grandeur and the elegance of large, theoretical, highbrow studies that appear to solve all problems except the specific one that evoked the study in the first place. Advertising men, in and out of research, want to fly before they can walk.

The irrationality of the marketplace and the lack of ability to specify what is good or bad advertising constitute a major source of job insecurity for the advertising man. If sales are up, it can be claimed (by the client) that they should be even higher. If sales are down, it can be claimed (by the agency) that only the advertising kept them from going even lower. Since no one "really knows," skill at persuasion, at use of pressure tactics, at politics, and at "human relations" becomes as important in gaining and keeping an account as the "objective reality."

The organizational and personnel problem this presents is decisive. Since the client is the source of all benefits to the agency and its personnel, and since agency personnel are usually better paid than officials in corresponding positions in the client firm, the burden of proof of the agency's efficiency is placed on the agency.

It is unusual when client personnel do not resent the "excessive salaries," the glamorous expense account, and the claims of infallibility that agencies make in their initial solicitation for an account. Their resentment is expressed in excessive demands upon the agency. Tight deadlines, impossible work loads, and unreasonable tasks are presented to the agency as a matter of course. This is often expressed in the phenomenon of the "exercise." The client will present a real or hypothetical marketing or advertising problem to the agency. A short deadline is given, and the implicit or explicit threat is made that retention of the account requires a satis-

00852

factory solution to the problem. The agency personnel are
then compelled to work day and night, weekday and week-
end, under fantastic costs of money, time, and energy to
prove the agency worthy of keeping the account. After all the
work is done and the agency has demonstrated its loyalty by
dancing to the client's tune, the final report is frequently left
unread for weeks or filed away without ever having been
read. The agency has, for the time being, paid for the commissions it earns from the largesse of the lower-paid client. In
rare instances agencies will resign accounts because of the
physical or mental breakdown of key personnel (lower-ranking personnel count less) or because the excessive demands
by one client prevent their giving full attention to other, more
profitable or less demanding accounts.

The philosophy of the exercise and the attitudes it engen-
ders in agency management are major determinants of relationships within the agency. This is precisely so because the
anxiety, powerlessness, and pressure placed upon the agency
and its personnel by clients are linked to the extremes of
success and failure that are possible because of labor-intensity, the claims for infallibility, and the inability to measure
successful advertising.

THE OCCUPATIONAL AND SKILL
STRUCTURE OF THE AGENCY

THE AGENCY, to repeat, is a service industry that provides in-
tangible skills and counsel to a manufacturing or marketing
company. Its product, advertising, is not a standardized
product that is mass-produced and sold at low cost to a large
number of widely distributed consumers. On the contrary, the
final product of the agency—a radio or TV commercial, a
print advertisement or a billboard—is made in somewhat the
same way as any other piece of art. The difference between
genuine art and advertising (as production and not as aesthetics) is that advertising art involves committee planning,

consultation, strategy, research, and the coordination of a wide variety of artistic and nonartistic specialists. The former include writers, audio technicians, painters and graphic men, photographers, engravers, cameramen (cinematic or still), musicians, animators, film editors, TV directors, stage designers, and producers. Art in advertising thus may resemble art in architecture or art under a patronage system in which the patron and his minions determine a great deal of the content and execution of the final art product.

Perhaps the only routine and semiautomatic work in advertising is in typing, billing, and other clerical work. Production work in the sense of semiskilled or unskilled factory work is almost entirely absent. As estimated earlier, almost 40 percent of total agency personnel are engaged in creative, administrative, professional, or high-level staff work. While it is true that there is a wide variety of higher skills assembled in one relatively small enterprise (six hundred to seven hundred people), it is also true that the number of people who professionally exercise any one skill is relatively small.

The account supervisor is a man whose major responsibility is to represent the agency to the client, to receive instructions from the client, to make agency recommendations to the client, to coordinate the efforts of the agency in preparing plans and advertising for the client. The account supervisor is in charge of over-all supervision of the account and is concerned with policy, while the account executive is placed in charge of administering the internal operation of the agency as it relates to a particular client.

Working for and with the account supervisor and executive is the account group. The account group consists of creative, technical, and staff specialists, media planners and buyers, researchers, merchandisers, and sales-promotion men. Each account group thus is a miniature advertising agency that has a full range of specialists attached to it and is capable of rendering a complete servicing of the account. There are as many account groups in an agency as there are accounts. When the account is a large one, the staff assigned to that account may be employed exclusively on the account in question. When the account is a small one, members of an account group may divide their time between a number of accounts.

Thus the agency usually has a double organization. One set of "bosses" consists of the account supervisor and executive. The other set consists of the heads of individual departments, that is, research director, copy chief or creative director, media director, art director, and so on. Each set of "bosses" has the same employees, and each set has at times different vested interests in the distribution of its employees' time and efforts. The overall agency officers—the president and chairman of the board—are the referees when conflicts occur, and the board of directors offers the formal representation of the various vested interests of both types. Their meetings are the official stage where conflicts are acted out and, if possible, resolved.

Typical conflicts are as follows:

1. When account personnel work on more than one account, their account supervisors may feel that the "part-time" help are spending too much time on other accounts. The account supervisors almost always feel that their account is understaffed. In terms of pressures on the account supervisor, this is probably true.

2. The "part-time" staff usually feel that account supervisors are too demanding. Instead of having two, three, or four part-time jobs, they feel they have that many full-time jobs.

3. The account supervisors quite often feel, especially if their account is not a huge or major one, that the creative and technical staff assigned to them are the rejects, misfits, and incompetents who have been assigned to their account on the basis of lack of ability.

4. Most service personnel are technicians, artists, or specialists, while the account supervisor is either a "business administrator," with no specialized, creative knowledge, or an ex-specialist. As a result, the creative or technical specialist feels that nincompoops, politicians, and incompetents meddle unnecessarily in business they know nothing about. They tend to feel that incompetents among their own bosses and at the client's shop force them to do countless revisions of per-

fectly good work, or even force them to execute ideas that are
so badly conceived or undefined that perfect execution only
makes apparent the stupidity of the plans. Thus they feel that
most of the work done is totally unnecessary.

5. The account supervisors, on the other hand, feel that
the technical specialists are "purists," academicians—temper-
amental, obstreperous, and difficult. Moreover, they resent
the feeling that the technical and creative specialists communicate a sense of being superior and of treating the account
executive as if he were a dope.

6. Department heads resent the account heads, frequently
feeling that the latter make excessive demands for their accounts on department personnel. They tend to feel that account heads want to tell the service heads and personnel how
to do the work that the latter are especially qualified for.
They also feel that account heads, to save their own necks,
will risk the necks of the service personnel by forcing them to
do inferior, dishonest, or unnecessary work. They feel they
are obliged to be cat's-paws, rescuing the chestnuts from the
fire caused by the negligence and incompetence of account
heads.

7. The account heads reciprocate this feeling, justifying
their attitudes in terms of the jealousy and intransigence of
the heads of the service departments.

8. All the above conflicts are expressed quite often in
private gossip, in conflicts over salaries and over the amount
and availability of agency stock. The account executive feels
that he is the businessman whose job it is to deal with the
client, keep him happy, and keep the account in the shop. He
has to have tact, to lie, flatter, drink, eat, and live with stupid
people in order to keep an account. He must do this by being
self-effacing, polite, and deferential even under the pressures
of the conscious and unconscious needling and resentment of
the client. This entitles him to a lion's share of the rewards.

The technical or creative specialist feels that he does the
actual job of planning, creating, and executing the final
product (the advertisement) and/or its placement in a
medium. Since this is the manifest job of the agency, the
lion's share of the reward should be his.

9. In addition, each specialist group develops a special theory of advertising that just happens to make its function supreme. Copywriters insist that the slogan or apt phrase, the play on words, is the particular ingredient that sells a product. Art directors will stress the symbol and the mood as being especially creative of positive brand images that lead to sales. When images become passé, art directors may insist upon humorous animation. ("You can get across unprovable claims by exaggerating them so much that even if the viewer consciously disbelieves them, he unconsciously accepts them.")

Television producers sell "realistic" and "atmospheric" mood photography, montage effects, use of succession of still shots of puppets to produce "animation"—all techniques designed to transport the viewer out of his normal, hardheaded buying attitude into a world that, because of the suspension of belief, is more "real" than the real world, and within which buying the advertised brand is linked to the fulfillment of the viewer's idealized self-image. Thus the TV producer, too, can make a claim for greater salary and more stock on the basis of attainment of this ideal.

The research director knows no limits to his megalomania except those that he encounters in the resistances that all other departments offer to the inquisitive snooping of research. Research enables the research director to "know" the audience, the customer, the sales personnel, and to "know" the action that will lead to success. He can research everybody's area of competence except his own, and can thus tell everyone else how to do his work. Every other department is forced, in the face of the self-aggrandizing research director, either to limit the operations of research or to control them to serve the special purposes of that department.

Research *does,* however, sometime provide answers to specific questions, *does* provide an aura of knowing for the agency as a whole, is useful to specialists in providing them with viable alternatives, and is helpful to the account supervisor in keeping an account and to top management in acquiring accounts. This utility constitutes the claim of the research director and his department for higher salaries and a greater share of profits.

10. The assignment of technical and creative specialists to distinct and separate account groups has additional consequences. While all copywriters, for example, are members of the creative department, each copywriter actually works with only a few other copywriters on an account or group of accounts. He does not work with copywriters other than those assigned to his own account, though his office will be in the creative department, next to the offices of all other copywriters.

His working partners, aside from the few other copywriters on his team, are account heads, artists, television producers, media planners and buyers, researchers, and so on. Thus each specialist works primarily with other specialists who have different specialties from his own. Each is competent to judge only his own specialty, and each is required by the working relationship to make judgments about work he is not especially qualified to judge.

Since each has the vested interest of his craft, the trained incompetence, or the occupational psychosis that characterizes almost all specialists, each attempts if he can to impose his own perspective on his account group. But each specialist has some vested interests in his account group, as opposed to that of his service departmental peers. The value of his services is measured by the way his account group has served to attract and maintain clients. His claim for salary increase and stock benefits is in part related to the success of his account group. Thus each specialist at times competes against his occupational peers and his service department.

The pattern of using small numbers of occupational specialists on an account group, together with other types of occupational specialists, tends to isolate each from his peers, to turn specialists into rivals, and to cause them to compete with one another for greater income. Thus the fractionization of the agency into occupational specialties tends to be supplemented by a fractionization of each occupational specialty into account specialties. The individual specialist is thus almost always placed in a cross-pressure between specialty and account. In the short run, he might find it profitable to align himself with his account group. If he does this too obviously

or too defiantly, he may risk incurring the enmity of his
service department head or of his occupational peers. Thus
each service department head would like to insist on the
integrity and loyalty of his department in the face of continuous undermining by account supervision.

The competition within a service department is best illustrated by the "creative" competition when a new account
enters a shop or when the client requests a new campaign
("The old one is tired"). A number of creative groups
(copywriters and artists) are asked to prepare a series of
alternative campaigns. Each group is briefed in the background of the account, its past history, its overall marketing,
sales, and advertising strategy, and the relevant research
background. Each group is given a deadline, and each
group prepares prototype advertisements in semifinished form
that embody its creative effort. When the deadline has passed,
the prototype advertisements are judged by the account
supervisors, top agency management, and by the client. The
creative group that submits the campaign closest to the one
finally adopted usually is assigned to the account. Losers,
especially if they were previously assigned to the account in
question, are relegated to less important accounts. If one gets
the new account assignment, one has a further claim to income and prestige; if one loses too many competitions, one
becomes a drifter and is sooner or later forced to find another
job.

In such competitions, therefore, the tension is deadly. Each
creative group attempts to keep its major slogan, theme, or
strategy a secret, and some groups attempt to ferret out the
secrets of other groups in order to steal them, modify them,
or develop, by implication only, a neutralizing theme or anti-
dote. Each creative group attempts to "lobby" for its campaign, even though the campaign may exist only as a glimmer
in a copywriter's eye; and each may attempt to influence any
department that is to evaluate or judge the competition. All
relevant parties are drawn into the competition, and each is
used as a tool, even if heedless, of the aspirations of the
competing creative groups.

This competition is only an extreme illustration of the
normal competition between occupational peers. To some ex-

tent such normal competition exists within all departments, and each department member is thus isolated from his peers. To be sure, temporary alliances do exist, based upon common assignments in the present or upon the prospects of profitable assignments in the future. But each man knows that his organizational position can change overnight, that his friends can become his enemies, and vice versa. Thus to walk carefully and watchfully is a *sine qua non* of handling oneself.

11. Since all departments have their sets of rival theories and claims for functional indispensability, the adjudication of such claims is the central function of generalized management.

Advertising agencies organize, disorganize, and reorganize constantly in order to solve the problem of control. In some agencies account supervision is dominant; in others, service departments have major responsibility; and in still others, one service department may be supreme. In the latter case, the agency may be known as a "research agency," an "artwork agency," a "copy agency," specializing in either "hard-sell" or mood commercials. Other agencies, usually the colossi, sell "total advertising," or total marketing, a claim for excellence in all departments and in all services.

A second function of agency management is to control the account groups. If the account supervisor becomes too strong and has complete control of the client's affections and billings, he can either "blackjack" the agency or walk off with the account. The agency president, board chairman, and service departments are thus forced to develop independent channels of communication to the client that limit the influence of the account supervisor.

SKILL REQUIREMENTS FOR
AGENCY PERSONNEL

To be successful in agency work, artists, copywriters, designers, and other creative personnel need to be talented, trained in the exercise of their skill, and, if possible, creative.

Talent and training are attributes that can be judged (if not measured) by qualified experts, if these are available. Creativity in advertising can be judged only under pressure, if it can be judged at all.

A talented copywriter, without ideas, can go far if he is able to develop the necessary appearances of creativity. Thus when the "Be sociable, have a Pepsi" idea made Pepsi-Cola a major competitor of Coca-Cola, hundreds of brands in all product classes launched advertising that pictured the consumers of these brands as young, modern, carefree, sophisticated, fun-loving, sociable, prosperous, upper-middle-class suburbanites. This image became in a short time a cliché but a highly successful cliché—successful in raising the unspoken wishes of millions of Americans into a self-conscious "model for the millions." The cliché had such wide distribution and penetration that those copywriters and agencies who indiscriminately copied it were not able to establish any distinguishing characteristics for the brands they advertised.

To copy early in the copying cycle may be profitable; to copy late is suicidal. To copy a campaign that is so old that everybody has forgotten it may be a stroke of near genius. To create a genuine concept, a totally new idea that works, requires as much creativity in advertising as it does in other fields of art, letters, and sciences. Unfortunately, the collective character of the creative enterprise in advertising, and the speed at which both good and bad ideas are copied, make it almost impossible to recognize the original creator.

It is relatively easy to judge the skills of technicians in research, in film editing, in audio departments, in camera work, because there are established techniques in these fields. But even in technical fields the mechanical application of technique results in dull, plodding work. Insight, imagination, the ability to apply technique to the solution of a "business" or aesthetic problem require, even in advertising, the same kinds of artistry that are required of creative personnel. And in these aspects of the work, the criteria for judging a man's work become just as subjective as those used for judging the creative artist.

Media planners, time and space buyers, and buyers of television programs usually develop a great deal of detailed knowledge of their respective fields merely by working in them. No special training is required of the neophyte to enter the field. But once he is in such a field, special talents for detail work, administration, and ability to exercise "good business judgment" are qualities that bring a good man to the fore.

These nontechnical business and administrative requirements resemble those appropriate to the account. The account executive and supervisor are required to be "good businessmen," good administrators, and to have "good business judgment." In addition, the account administrators are required to be tactful, likable, charming, and to have, to a very high degree, all the qualities of successful salesmen. The similarity in the personal qualities required of the media buyer and the account man frequently results in the promotion of the time and space buyer to account executive, thence to account supervisor, and finally to agency president.

This career pattern is not fixed. Creative personnel, research men, media men, and a wide variety of other occupational types can become account executives; and all types can become agency presidents. But if a specialist is to become an account supervisor or an agency president, he must first exhibit the qualities of the general administrator, businessman, and man of judgment. He has the opportunity to develop these qualities as a department head and administrator, as a member of the board of directors, or in making an impression on important representatives of the client in agency-client meetings or at lunch and after-hours meetings.

Yet a description of the above qualities does not come near to setting forth all the qualities necessary to success in occupational mobility. As indicated above, talent and technical knowledge are desirable qualities for creative and technical personnel. But possession of such qualities results only in the acquisition of rank and position as a staff official. Administrative skill, judgment, and business sense are the terms used to describe the special talents of the nonspecialized business men of the agency, who include media and program buyers, account executives and supervisors, and general agency officials. Such lists of qualifications, however, represent only the *public* side of an occupational description. Other, more personal qualities are necessary to complete the description.

Nerve is a central quality that any agency man must possess in order to survive the pressures. Since much of agency work is done under the constant pressure of volume, deadlines, possible criticism, and the ever-present image of total failure, men who cannot "stand the grind" are quickly recognized. Those who can are selected as "comers" and are pushed along as long as they can keep the respect of those who do the pushing.

Nerve means more than the failure to crack under pressure. It means the capacity to exhibit, regardless of the pressures placed on one, calmness, tact, proper deference, good humor, and loyalty to the right people. But these latter qualities are independent of nerve. The ability to exhibit calmness, tact, deference, good humor, and loyalty to the right people is considered to be a basic personality requirement for any account officer, agency officer, or any creative or technical specialist who wants to move upward. For these qualities are client-pleasing qualities. They are also boss-pleasing qualities. Being in a business where one's very existence depends on the "favors" bestowed on one by the client gives advertising a courtlike atmosphere. The chief officer of the client is the "king," and the agency personnel are only one set of his courtiers. But the courtiers on each level, by virtue of their acceptance by the throne and by individuals who have access to the throne, receive deference in relationship to their imputed proximity to the throne. Ability to be successful as a courtier becomes objectified, is treated as a psychological trait in and of itself, and becomes the basis for further success in courtsmanship.

The quality of likability (other-orientedness with a purpose) is subject to limitations. In a business where costs are a factor, where pressures are greater than one can absorb by oneself, the ability to resist pressures which are destructive to the individual is a necessary trait for success and for survival. For instance, a client may make demands that are too expensive, too time-consuming, or are impossible of fulfillment.

The account executive in this case must either talk the client into modifying his demands or convince him that his demands have been fulfilled when they have not. At times he may be able to convince the client that the demands are totally unreasonable. But whatever he does, the account executive must do so in a manner that gains the respect or the liking of the client. If the account executive gives in to such demands, he may embarrass the agency and its profit structure, overload the technical, administrative, and creative staffs who have to meet the demands, and find himself in trouble with his own bosses. Moreover, if the account executive indicates to the client that he can be pushed around, he invites the resentful or sadistic client to do just that. Finally, some clients expect top agency personnel to have convictions, policies, and beliefs of their own. They are paid to have these attributes. The account executive who is so likable that he accedes to whatever the client wishes is simply not doing his job. He is not providing the client with the counsel which is part of the service of the agency. If he does disagree, however, he must be tactful and, above all, he must know when to stop disagreeing. This *realistic toughness* is the third major quality necessary for success in an agency.

The three major personality traits so far discussed become the basis for types of agency personnel. The types are as follows:

Type 1. THE CREATIVE GENIUS. This is the official who creates or attempts to create the impression that his technical knowledge or creative ability is so great that he can ignore the other realities of the agency business. If he succeeds (by being almost as good as he claims to be), he can go far toward a top staff position. He is usually viewed as irresponsible in positions that require "judgment" or administrative ability.

Type 2. THE LIKABLE CHAP. He works hard and is continually on the run. He is pleasing, amiable, entertaining, and quite frequently provides more services than the client or account supervisor asks for. He is perfectly eager and willing to handle all details for his superiors, or to get someone else to do so. But he is at a total loss when two or more superiors disagree, or when he is asked to have an opinion before an official opinion exists. He lacks nerve. Such a person is not likely to reach a position higher than account executive because he finds it difficult to work without lines and because he is likely to give away his own, his subordinates', and, worse, the agency's shirt in the desire to please. He needs to work under Type 3.

Type 3. THE TOUGH REALIST. He may not have creative or technical ability but knows how to please when that quality is necessary. He knows when to get tough with his subordinates, with himself ("discipline"), and with the client. He knows in any given situation what his self-interest is, what the client's interests are, and what the agency's, account group's, or service department's interests are. No matter what the social situation is, he knows how to juggle these interests so that he, in the final analysis, will come out on top. Of course, such results do not always occur. When two or more tough realists come into open conflict, one may be forced to go (even if this means his occupational demise). One can make an error in judgment, such as cultivating and supporting an important official in the client firm, only to discover later that this "personal" client has been squeezed out. The enemies of the personal client may now be running the client firm, and the agency man is *persona non grata.* If this happens, the tough realist may be out of a job. A tough realist may spend a decade cultivating a particular individual in the client firm, nursing him up the ladder of success in his own firm. Shortly after the client "arrives," he dies. The tough realist then loses his "contact" and may have no other assets of value when he faces his own agency.

The three types can be conceived of as polar types. Most personnel in an agency, however, exhibit combinations of the traits of the three polar types. The creative genius can also be a likable chap or a tough realist (if he is willing to suppress his needs for personal recognition), but he cannot be both. The likable chap is likely to be a pure type. However, a likable account executive, after achieving that position, may

suddenly begin to sound like a tough realist. If he can maintain that attitude under pressure or adversity, he may grow up
to be a genuine tough realist. The tough realist may have had,
in the earlier years of his career, creative or technical ability
which, by and large, he is not able to exercise in the present
because of the pressures of other work. He can always be
likable when necessary. But the quality that accounts for his
success is his realistic toughness.

THE "MEANING OF WORK" IN AN ADVERTISING AGENCY

OUR DISCUSSION of the economic, occupational, social, and
psychological structure of the advertising agency defines
much of what can be said of the "meaning of work" in an
agency, for the very framework and operation of the agency
constitute a set of limitations and opportunities for the individual. What these limitations and opportunities are to a
particular individual is a function of the nature of the social
structure within which he works, his particular needs, motivation, and personality, and the particular way his personality
is linked to that social structure.

The phrase "meaning of work" is an ambiguous term.
"Meaning" can be conceived of as the immanent set of meanings that attach to an *objective* event, situation, or social
structure. In this sense work can be conceived of as being
meaningful in and of itself, without the support of external
rewards and gratifications which are a product of the work
but are not in the work. This immanent meaning can be
contrasted to instrumental meanings in which the "meaning"
(the satisfaction one gets from the work) is not in the work
itself but in what the work enables one to do in other areas of
life. Thus dull routine or painful work, work that contains no
joy, can be meaningful if, by doing it, one achieves an economic gain, prestige, power, or even the perfection of a skill
that is useful for the attainment of some other goal. With

these distinctions in mind we can pose the question: What are the internal and external meanings attached to work in an advertising agency?

It is simplest to discuss external meaning. As we have previously indicated, advertising work is extremely well paid, has tremendous opportunities for mobility, and in a high-tax economy offers a capable man great opportunities to acquire wealth. Such economic motivations need not necessarily imply that the advertising man is a crass materialist. The acquisition of wealth, in a society that is heir to the Protestant ethic, is simply a means for a man to legitimate himself in terms of the only standards that may be meaningful to him. Certainly economic and social mobility through success in advertising may mean to an individual that he is on his way to fulfilling the American dream. His efforts, his manhood, his ideals are affirmed by his success. The successful man can hold his head up high in his community and can gain the respect of his wife, friends, and neighbors if they happen to share his dream. He develops confidence, poise, assertiveness, and even arrogance in his relationships with others outside the industry, no matter how timid and "likable" he is in the agency. Moreover, the upwardly mobile agency man earns almost sufficient income to acquire a lifestyle that conforms to his image of what middle- and upper-class life is like. He can play at being a solid citizen, an upper bohemian, or an English-type country squire. Each type of play is a further affirmation of his version of the American dream and therefore must be taken seriously. But mobile advertising men are usually intelligent, articulate, educated, and expert at seeing through false appearances, including their own. They have this ironic talent because they are marginal men and because their occupational selection and function require them to construct "artificial worlds" which can enchant and seduce outsiders. This talent for analysis cannot be "turned off" when it comes to the analysis of oneself. Thus in playing the solid citizen, the upper bohemian, or the English country squire, advertising men tend to burlesque themselves, doing so half with tongue in cheek and half seriously. This comic aspect of one's private life is frequently presented to friends in the profession, but a more serious demeanor is presented to outsiders.

The thousands of jokes about advertising men, the satires of the language of advertising ("Let's put it [an idea] on at New Haven and see where it gets off," or, "Let's get down on our hands and knees and look at it from the client's point of view") are inventions of successful advertising men who cannot genuinely understand their own success because that success appears to be based on so little. Self-deprecation is one of the prices one pays for what is thought of as unearned success.

Part of this ironical attitude, which is based on the notion of "pinch me—it may not be so," derives from the fact that it may not be "so" tomorrow, for the mobile advertising man realizes, perhaps not openly, that a single job failure at the age of forty-five or over by a man with a salary of $20,000 and over may make it all "not so." Thus he can never accept fully, at all levels of his consciousness, the success he might otherwise believe in. To outsiders he may act the role of the successful executive. To the few insiders whom he feels he does not have to "sell," he may confide his anxieties or ironies. The anxieties emerge in pressure-cooker situations, and the ironies in success situations.

An additional set of supporting external meanings is found in the idea that the advertising man makes important decisions for big companies, representing hundreds of millions of dollars of annual sales or billions of dollars of corporate wealth. The young advertising executive, and even an older one, may confide to his wife or friend that he sat in a meeting with the president of a giant corporation and perhaps even said something. He may point to a commercial that is on the air, and say: "See that commercial? I wrote one line of it!" or he may say in irony: "I recommended against it." He can speak knowingly about the inner affairs of gigantic American corporations to his male friends, or speak even more knowingly about soaps, detergents, floor polishes, foods, and sauces to his wife and his wife's friends. When "the business of America is business," being close to business and to the thrones of the monarchs of business is enchanting.

To the successful advertising man who is himself the son of a successful father, success in advertising has different meanings. Success means the validation of one's birthright, the proof that one has lived up to the task handed down by one's father or family. Success, then, is both a right and a duty; failure is a disgrace. The upper-class advertising man is less likely to develop the ironic self-mockery of the upwardly mobile man. He is likely to take the surrealistic atmosphere of advertising seriously, to accept its rituals, and act unselfconsciously. He is likely to be reliable in dealing with clients because he does not let the mask slip; he has no mask. Therefore he is capable of genuine sincerity in an industry where sincerity is a major stock-in-trade. The sincere upper-class advertising man is not likely to understand the ironic, sardonic, and self-deprecating mobile man. He feels that such a man will befoul his own nest, will risk upsetting the client, and will regard him as being "thick" or stupid.

These mutual feelings of lack of admiration, however, are usually not expressed; they are kept behind the façades of deference and authority that reflect the respective positions of the individuals in question. Occasionally they are expressed directly; more often they are expressed between two individuals of similar class and occupational position. Most often they result from the fact that individuals of diverse backgrounds do not understand each other.

A third external meaning of advertising work comes from the enjoyment of the glamour of advertising. This includes enjoyment of the food and drink in fancy restaurants, the enjoyment being more a function of the expense than the quality of the food, the drink, or the company. The idea of air travel, with sudden and long trips for short conferences, stays at expensive hotels, and living on the expense account all make life exciting when discussed with outsiders or with the less fortunate. One quickly becomes an authority on exotic foods, restaurants, hotels, and cities, and can compare notes with the equally fortunate. The glamour of advertising supports the feeling of success that mobility may bring, and it sometimes provides a substitute for more tangible success. Most pathetically, one frequently hears of newly graduated college students who, in applying for an advertising job, cite as their reason the glamour of the job, as well as the economic opportunities or the chance to come close to what they regard as the sources of power and the throne.

Another form of external meaning can come from acceptance of the public ideology. Hypothetically, this meaning pattern would be stated as follows: "Advertising is a service not to me personally or to the clients only, but to the economy as a whole. It keeps the economy going, creates new products, new jobs, makes industry competitive, and helps to bestow the advantages of free enterprise on our economy." This ideology is the basis for the theme and rhetoric of after-dinner speeches, interviews with and articles by distinguished leaders of the advertising industry, advertising and marketing professors, and industrialists speaking or writing for public consumption.

We have described this service ideology as a hypothetical system of meaning. It is hypothetical because it represents a possibility but not an actuality. Advertising men simply do not speak in these terms in personal conversation. At most, a top official will utter such sounds in an informal group when he is practicing for a speech or writing a paper for public consumption. If he does this among his peers, they are likely to interject wry comments. They may well document his speech with examples of conspicuous waste, stupidity, or mismanagement, conducted either by advertising men or by their clients. Even upper-class top officials who take advertising seriously are not likely to indulge in "speech-making" in intimate circles, if only to avoid such wry comment.

On the contrary, most advertising men compile and treasure the conspicuous boners, the waste and fatuousness that advertisers and their agencies commit. Stories are circulated about the most sensational television buy of the decade, bought by a company that was so late in reaching a buying decision that it had to buy the only show available, against its inclinations—a show that all other companies and agencies who had been offered it had turned down. Other such stories concern the successful man who moves upward and onward by ruining everything he touches; the company that re-

searches a product so long and so well that, by the time it is
done with its research, its competitors have preempted the
market; the company whose advertising and marketing policies and operations can be turned into a casebook on how not
to advertise or market a brand. Advertising men have discussed the Cold War with the hope that the Russians have a
number of marketing and advertising men in their top ranks
to balance the odds a little. It is hoped that the Russians can
foul up at least as often as American industry.

Ideology, as it is publicly expressed, then, does not provide
meaning in the sense that such meaning may sustain the
motivations of individuals. At best it provides a claim for the
respectability and legitimacy of the industry, a claim made by
individuals who do not believe the claim in any operative
sense. Very few advertising men, however, will deny in public
the ideology of advertising. To do so would rock the boat,
result in a public squabble, and invite clients to withdraw
their advertising from agencies that employ controversial
characters.

The operative external meanings of work can be conceived
of as those surrounding economic gain, and the glamour and
self-importance achieved by working in an important industry, and not by an ideology of service.

INTERNAL MEANINGS IN ADVERTISING

As PREVIOUSLY INDICATED, internal meanings derive from
joy in performing an activity for the sake of the activity itself,
and not for the external products of that activity. At first
glance, this category of meaning appears to be most applicable to creative personnel and to technologists. The writer, the
artist, the designer, the musical composer, the trained researcher—all enter the agency with specialized interests, talents, and training in their respective fields. Working in advertising gives the artist or technologist an opportunity to be
paid for exercising his creative ability, his craft, or his specialized methodology on "real, live problems" where his art and
science can have some effect.

If this is the hope that brings a talented individual into advertising, he is doomed to quick disappointment. For the creative artist or technologist discovers almost immediately that advertising writing, art, and science are not for the small magazine, the gallery, or the scientific journal (except marketing journals). The problems he works on are selected by others. The strategy he works on is the product of countless, boring meetings with artistic or scientific nincompoops. At each stage of his work, the Philistines make suggestions and otherwise interfere. When a work is done, the Philistines reject the already compromised mess because it does not meet the specifications they were unaware of when they commissioned the work. So back he goes to the drawing board to start all over again under much the same conditions.

The creative man or technologist begins to arrive at a genuine understanding of advertising when he realizes that his work is a tool, a means of achieving goals that lie outside the work itself. Such goals consist of getting the job done on time in a manner that is satisfactory to someone else (if not to his former self), of helping his boss, his department, his agency, and his client to do the job they were assigned, and of getting properly rewarded for successful completion of his work. All these meanings may be admirable, but frequently they are meanings that an individual discovers after he has been in advertising for some time, and after he has been disappointed or broken in the attempt to do what he regards as more creative, scientific, or serious work.

Individuals who enter advertising with less grandiose aspirations are less likely to be disenchanted, but they are also less likely to do creative work in advertising. This is because even burned-out ideals and creativity, when not accompanied by bitterness, allow the creative or scientific technician to approach the creation of an advertisement with some of the talent, sensitivity, and techniques that a dedicated artist and scientist can bring to noncommercial work.

Thus the exposure to agency work tends to turn internal meanings into external meanings. Work tends to lose its meaning-for-itself and to develop instrumental meanings.

There are, of course, limitations to this process. A major limitation consists in the persistence of the "instinct for workmanship," pride in craftsmanship, in doing a sound, workman-like job. Pride in craftsmanship appears to be as central to the personality of a creative individual as any other trait. It is the last quality to disappear. Thus most creative and scientific personnel will continue to strive for technical excellence in their work regardless of whether they think the work they are asked to do is badly conceived, is inartistic or unscientific, or essentially is not their own. More conflicts between creative and noncreative personnel take place over techniques than over aesthetics or over ethics. This is because technical virtuosity is the last remnant of a man's pride in his creative ability. To the layman or to a specialist in another field, it is a source of considerable amusement, and at times ennui, to see two creative specialists or technicians fighting tooth and nail (but politely) over minor points of technique that do not appear to affect the strategy, overall design, or imputed results of an advertisement. However, such concern for detail usually results in technically accomplished advertising.

For the noncreative, nontechnical person in advertising, there should, at first appearance, be no internal meaning to his work. His job is primarily administrative in nature. It involves keeping track of the flow of paper through channels, and accelerating, stopping, or restarting that flow. It involves "selling" to superiors and clients, and manipulating, planning, coaxing, and coercing cooperation and work out of inferiors and peers. He comes to such tasks with no particular interest, talent, or creative genius. By and large, his motivations for getting into the field are: it pays well, it sounds glamorous and exciting, and there is nothing else he really wants to do. Once he becomes an advertising man, he really discovers all the opportunities for advancement, the excitement and the glamour and the possibilities for failure, the pressures, the overwork, the conspiracies, the powerlessness, the isolation, and the anxiety that are recurrent in the course of his career.

Gentle personalities are likely to get out of advertising at relatively young ages. If they are "businessmen," they will try to move to large corporations where, at lower levels and at lower pay, the pressures and crises are less frequent and less turbulent. If they have merchandisable talents, they may try teaching, government, or some other stable field. This process of interindustry mobility results in a shakedown, leaving as survivors those who think they have nerve, toughness, talent, or other personal qualities necessary for the life of a courtier. Those who discover that they do not have these qualities, or do not have enough of them to maintain a career after they are well started on that career, are the genuine tragedies in advertising. They may be too successful to get out, but not strong enough to stay in. Individuals in this situation are the ones who break under pressure.

But to the strong, the nervy, the talented and tough, the very fact of pressure constitutes the strongest set of internal meanings possible. For the difficulties, the pressure, the politics and manipulation, the irrationality, the powerlessness, and the isolation all constitute a challenge to one's manhood. The challenge is "be crushed or survive." The answer the advertising man gives is: "Throw everything you can at me—work, pressure, senselessness—and somehow I will lick you and force you to throw even more work at me. Each victory will make me more able to survive new challenges, since my nerve and toughness will be greater and my skills will have been tested in more encounters." The response is a Promethean challenge to the gods and the fates.

The satisfaction involved is a sense of delight in knowing that one has succeeded in manipulating others, of "selling" the bosses or the client, defying the gods and the fates. If nerve and realistic toughness are the supremely valued traits of the tough realist, then awareness of one's exhibition and possession of these traits becomes a value in and of itself. Income, stock ownership, even the glamour of advertising and the way of life deriving from advertising, are merely external affirmations of an inner attitude. The inner attitude, not the results, is the chief value that excites the driving, tough businessman.

In a literary or philosophical imagery this meaning pattern can be called "Faustian." The Faustian man seeks goals outside himself that are difficult. His inner goals are to master the difficult, not to possess the goal, and to exercise his strength and talent in overcoming the obstacles. It is the feeling of strength, confidence, pride in mastery, and the recognition he gets from others for his ability that constitute the source of his joy in work.

In psychological terms, this meaning pattern can be called narcissism. It is an intensified form of self-love because the satisfactions derived from activity are a self-conscious pride in achievement. The narcissistic individual, even in the midst of the most difficult work and pressure, keeps an area of his consciousness detached from his work. He becomes his own observer, checking on himself and commenting on his performance, as he manipulates himself and others. He works in a frenzy, and praises or condemns himself as he does so. In the sense that the detached observer in him robs him of the capacity to feel anything spontaneously, none of his feelings are "genuine." Even if he acts or speaks spontaneously, the narcissistic observer makes an ironic or detached analytical commentary on the action, saying, "Nicely done, boy," or, "You'll have to do better next time."

The driving ambition of the narcissist, then, is to win the plaudits of his own inner cheering stand. When he does so, the psychological tone he exhibits is euphoria, brazen self-confidence, aggressiveness, and optimism. When he fails, the psychological tone is depression, self-pity, paranoia, and feelings of rejection. But since the narcissist is self-conscious, he knows that if he can generate the attitudes of self-confidence, euphoria, and aggressiveness, he is likely to sound sincere, convincing, and effective.

Thus one of the most humorous and charming situations in advertising occurs when an account supervisor and his minions are about to make a presentation to the client. After all the work has been done, and the presentation, the charts, the film, the reports are all "locked up" and produced, several days are spent in meetings, rehearsals, and conversations during which each member of the team strokes up the enthusiasm and self-confidence of all others. Woe unto the hapless observer who wittingly or unwittingly discovers a flaw in operation or throws cold water on it. He destroys the self-confidence of the team, their enthusiasm, sincerity, and capacity for doing effective work. Collective narcissism is a necessary ingredient for teamwork.

Narcissism has other advantages for the advertising man. The source of narcissism is the basic energy of the individual. But with narcissism, all the energy is turned inward and becomes self-love. The individual gives this energy to himself and tells himself to use it in such a way that narcissism can grow and grow and grow. Thus the narcissist in his euphoric stages has immense reserves of energy, confidence, and aggressiveness that he can direct at narcissistic purposes. He can work at top speed under the worst of pressure for extended periods of time until he collapses either from failure or from physical and psychological fatigue. The demands, the pressures, that advertising work places on the advertising man, then, are appropriate to the narcissist.

However, the narcissistic energy evoked by the man and his job cannot be shut off at will. The energy once released needs an outlet, and will rattle and shake its owner if there is no outlet. In advertising, the flow of work is uneven; in between crises, storms, and drives there are sometimes extended periods of calm. After the individual has recovered his strength from the last crisis, any further period of calm becomes a threat. The restless energy wants to be released. Advertising men solve this problem in a number of ways. Severe measures to bottle up the energy can be taken at the risk of depression. Narcissistic energy can be released in drinking, entertaining, partying, carousing, and active and demanding vocations and sports. All these are parts of the way of life of many advertising men. Finally, if there is no crisis, one can always be provoked. This can be done consciously, by starting a new round of solicitations for new business; or it can be done unconsciously by starting a fight with a peer, the client, or another department. One can demand an "exercise" to keep one's subordinates busy; or one can feud and fuss out of lack of interest in routine, calm, peaceful work.

If narcissism is turned into useless burning of unnecessary energy, it becomes self-destructive. The individual wears himself out physically and emotionally, moves from crisis to

crisis, and, finally, from breakdown to breakdown. He dies
before his time. If he uses his narcissism to provoke crises,
feuds, self-dramatizing arguments and quarrels, the narcissist
can precipitate crises in others, causing conflict and resentments that can wreck an organization.

Narcissism is a generalized psychological trait that can
erupt in anyone. As such, it is not linked particularly to
advertising. Narcissism can be linked to any kind of work—it
merely means that one is preoccupied with the response to
one's self in work rather than with the work itself. Narcissism
is likely to be a dominant characteristic in the creative and
performing arts where the person releases tremendous energies to act more for an audience consisting of himself than for
the audience in the seats. It is likely to be present in politics
where the demands on the public personality are so great that
only an individual who enjoys his public performance can
endure the strain of that performance. It is also likely to be
found to a high degree in other industries where the occupational strains and stresses are similar to those of advertising.
These include public relations, the mass media, management
consulting, and the upper levels of all large-scale organizations.

But it is true that narcissism is found to a very great extent
in advertising. Why this should be so can be explained in
terms of the structure of advertising. Individuals with creative
talent or with scientific aspirations who are intrinsically interested in their work are driven out of the industry if they insist
that work be internally meaningful. If they remain in advertising, it is because their work has become instrumental to
them. To say that work is instrumental is to say that the work
becomes at the same time an object and a means for the
individual. The man is separated from his work by self-con-
sciousness, narcissism. Advertising thus makes narcissists out
of nonnarcissists.

In the same way, the noncreative businessman finds that
tremendous pressures, difficulties, obstacles, and anxieties are
placed in the path of achieving substantial but extrinsically
meaningful rewards. The pressures are so great that those
who cannot take them leave. Those who remain are the ones

who thrive on work and pressure, who enjoy work and pressure for what these enable them to accomplish. Those who remain are the narcissists.

Thus advertising modifies and selects personalities so that a few predominant types are produced. To the extent that advertising has the public image of being glamorous, exciting, close to the source of power, and frenzied, it attracts individuals who think they might survive in this atmosphere. Even the negative image of advertising serves as a recruiting poster to those who find the "negative image" positive. In this sense advertising recruits potential or actual narcissists as well as selecting and creating narcissists out of those who unwittingly enter its domain.

PERSONAL ETHICS IN ADVERTISING

MUCH OF OUR PREVIOUS DISCUSSION frames the discussion of the role of ethics in advertising. The word "ethics," however, is an ambiguous term. For our present purposes, "ethics" does not include the following:

1. Rules and regulations governing the competition between agencies, involving such "crimes" as account stealing, speculative unsolicited presentations to secure a new account, and raiding of personnel. We abstain from such discussion because we are concerned with personal ethics rather than with institutional or trade-association policies.

2. For the same reasons we are not concerned with the law, FTC, USDA, and FCC regulations per se. The extent to which individuals regard the law as a barrier to their personal goals is, of course, of some interest.

3. We are not concerned with ethics in an absolute sense, as perhaps expressed by the Golden Rule. The Golden Rule is too severe a standard to judge any industry by, and would not distinguish one industry from another. However, very few people in Western civilization can discuss ethics without having in the "back of the mind" the Judeo-Christian concept of ethics. For our present discussion we shall leave such ethics

in the back of the mind, allowing them to emerge when and where they must.

The operational definition of ethics we are forced to use is as follows: Those actions or rules for action which, when violated, produce in the violator, a spectator, or a person informed of the action, a sense of moral shock, disgust, or horror. The reverse of this definition also applies: Ethics are not operative when an "expected sense of horror" does not follow the commission or the knowledge of the action. In short, an action is viewed as ethical when it does not produce a negative judgment on moral grounds. It is viewed as unethical when it does.

ETHICS IN DEALING WITH THE PUBLIC

SINCE THE ECONOMIC FUNCTION of advertising is to help a manufacturer sell his brand, the evaluation of ethics might start with a consideration of what advertising men believe is ethical or unethical in the claims, promises, and techniques they use toward this end.

Complaints by Newton Minow and the FTC have revealed to the public that a great deal of "fraudulent" advertising is central to the day-to-day operations of the agency and its clients. Fake demonstrations appear in the commercials; fraudulent claims are made; misleading statements are presented as statistical facts. Product weaknesses are covered over—in fact, made into virtues. Any reading of FTC circulars, newspapers, or speeches by Newton Minow would reveal that part of the day-to-day fraud that government officials can discover as meeting the legal definitions of fraud.

Our discussion hinges not on the fact that fraudulent or misleading advertising exists but on the attitude of agency personnel to commercials that might be construed as fraudulent.

Agency personnel recognize as primary their economic function to help their client sell his brand. Anything that helps is useful, even fraudulent or misleading advertising. This is especially true if the brand has no unusual characteristics to make it attractive to the public. The copywriter or the account executive can paraphrase Winston Churchill, and say, "It is not my duty to preside at the liquidation of my client." This is all the more true if the advertised product is inferior to other brands. For in such cases, the copywriter's pride in craftsmanship is invoked ("Anybody can sell a product that sells itself, but it takes art to sell an inferior product"). Thus if a hairdressing is too greasy, one inverts the weakness by saying, "A little dab will do you . . . or the girls will pursue you." If the major cleaning ingredient in your client's detergent is so ineffective that it requires twice as much of that ingredient to equal the cleaning ability of the major competitor, you claim "twice the active cleaning ingredients." If your brand needs two or more ingredients to do the work that other products do with one ingredient, you advertise "twin-power" or "just like a doctor's prescription." If your product was inferior and a minor change has been made to make it almost equal to its competitors, you advertise it as "new," "improved," or "25 percent better" (better than what is not specified). You might add just enough of a "miracle" ingredient (lanolin, hexachlorophene, olive oil, and so on) to be able to advertise the ingredient but not enough to affect the cost or the product quality. You might even study the manufacturing process and discover a standard ingredient of all brands in the product class which no one has yet advertised, and then proceed, by advertising, to transform this into a new "miracle" ingredient. ("It has sixty-four beans in a cup.")

You may employ your research department to use technically accurate and honest surveys that lead, because of the glories of an ambiguous English language and grammar, to "dishonest" conclusions: "80 percent of all doctors prescribe the *ingredients* in our brand" (but the vast majority do not recommend the brand—in fact, may recommend against using the brand). Questionnaires are designed so that only one answer is possible, and subsequent research work is as scrupulously honest; the results are impeccable, and are used to provide the legal basis for an advertising claim.

At each point in this process, pride in craftsmanship enables the creative man to provide the client with "selling" advertising despite brand deficiences. Even when one has a brand that is technically superior, but whose superiority is the result of highly technical and difficult-to-understand features, it is frequently more efficient to develop a simple, fraudulent claim or demonstration than to demonstrate the difficult truth.

In all these cases, the primary criterion for advertising honesty is not the honesty or dishonesty of the advertising but its imputed selling efficiency.

So far as one can tell, advertising men do not object to telling these "necessary" lies. In fact, when the necessary lie is a creative one, they take great pride in their ability to overcome the deficiencies of the product. Some indications of malaise, however, are found in the ironical ways in which they will recount their creative escapades. Ironical pride may indicate that, if they could not tell the truth, they at least did a good job of lying. Thus virtuosity in fraud becomes a virtue. For the most part, however, even the desire to commit fraud is limited to that which is necessary to sell the brand.

Quite frequently advertisers will be more interested in truth-telling than agency people, especially copywriters. First of all, since they are not copywriters, they do not get the aesthetic satisfaction, except vicariously, from producing the creative lie; and second, the client suffers more than an individual copywriter from being the object of an FTC cease-and-desist order. Such an order may be worth millions of dollars of negative advertising for a brand. To avoid such problems, a crew of high-priced agency, client, and media lawyers inspect all copy and certify its probable legality before finished advertisements are prepared. Such precautions are necessary. The creative man, if given full freedom, will at times generate such patently fraudulent advertising that only a lawyer can stop him. Such creativity, however, is relatively infrequent. Most copywriters are aware of the legal limitations and, if they are not sure of them, will consult the lawyers in advance.

Nevertheless, a few copywriters do get the reputation of being moral lepers; they love fraud for fraud's sake. Such individuals will rejoice in the complicated, tricky, aesthetically satisfying lie even when the truth might be a powerful selling proposition. The moral leper is spotted almost as soon as he joins the agency. His fantastic lies (both in copywriting and in personal relations) are told and retold by all others. He is a source of humor to those not directly involved in working with him, and a source of danger and chagrin to all others. He is a source of danger because, in risking legal action, he endangers the account. Moreover, everyone connected with the moral leper (and technically he is a psychopath) must attempt to avoid or repair the harm he does to the agency and to others. He therefore causes more work than he accomplishes. However, a psychopath can be a good copywriter if he is controlled. There are few limits to his fancy, his imagination, or his ability to beg, borrow, or steal ideas that may be useful.

But the moral leper is the deviant that defines the important, operative ethical norms for advertising. He establishes the boundaries that must not be crossed. If one does pass over, one receives moral disapprobation. In relation to the public, this norm can be stated as follows: *"Don't tell an unnecessary lie."* Necessary lies are acceptable because they are essential to fulfill the economic function of the agency. What is more, all advertising men tend to be conscious of the pressures that all other men work under. They are sympathetic to the individual who suffers from moral and ethical lapses in response to these pressures. They are totally unsympathetic to the individual who enjoys lying, or to the person who lies beyond what is structurally necessary. Thus, in a genuine sense, most advertising men are profoundly moral.

ETHICS IN DEALING WITH CLIENTS

THE CLIENT is the advertising man's sole source of bread and butter. In addition to being well aware of this fact, the advertising man has other images of the client, which include the following:

Most clients are stupid. It they weren't, they'd be working in agencies where they'd get paid more.

Most clients are technically incompetent.

Most clients are sadistic, or resentful of the agency man because of the latter's ability and salary.

Most clients are unreasonable and overdemanding. They also stick their noses into business they are not equipped to handle.

Most clients are hungry, thirsty, and vain. They need constant attention, flattery, and fake deference.

Most clients are ingrates. They will switch accounts for petty reasons, especially after the agency has done a superhuman job.

Most clients want the credit for work well done, and will blame the agency for their own mistakes.

Some clients are gullible fools, but these are nice people.

All the above images are not applied to all clients. In fact, each agency will have one or more clients whose personal qualities, business acumen, and administrative ability set so high a standard that all other clients look feeble in comparison.
These images set the stage for the discussion of client-focused ethics. The fundamental strategy of the agency is to make convincing its claim for distinctive agency superiority and indispensability in meeting the client's needs. Once one acquires the account, the initial argument plus its proof must be continuously demonstrated, even in the face of falling sales ("They could, under other circumstances, fall even faster").
Ethics in relationship to the client are based on the norm *"Don't ever tell a direct lie to the client."* This may not even be an ethical norm, since it is based on the assumption that

without the client's trust in one's basic honesty, no enduring client-agency relationship is possible. The norm is thus a pragmatic device to keep the account.

If we consider the rule as an ethical norm, however, another set of normative propositions follows. While one does not tell a lie to the client, one does not always have to tell the total truth. The agency's fundamental business requirement is to keep profitable accounts. Therefore, agency communications to the client tend to conceal negative aspects of agency operations—inefficiency, indecision, or lack of attention to his account because major attention has been given to other accounts. It is assumed that clients are big boys and that it is their problem to discover the negative aspects of the client-agency relationship, not the duty of the agency to inform on itself.

When an account is secure, however, the agency may criticize its own advertising, volunteer research results that are negative, or otherwise criticize its own operation, especially if the agency is immediately prepared to take protective action. Such self-criticism builds trust and forestalls client-originated criticism.

The deviant individuals in client-agency ethics are of two types. The *schlemiel* who reveals agency difficulties to the client (either by accident or as an attempt to curry favor) is a menace who cannot be kept around. The moral leper, on the other hand, who tells the client lies that are too big, risks creating a basic mistrust by allowing himself and the agency to be exposed as "defrauding" the client. He is the worse menace. Between these two extremes are the tough realists who know how and when to tell the truth.

The "tough realist" client is respected but feared because there is less need to manipulate him and less danger of a sudden disenchantment. The tough realist expects more and less of the agency at the same time. He does not ask for miracles, but he does ask for hard, creative work. A good agency can provide this without the necessity for deception.

THE ETHICS OF INTERPERSONAL
RELATIONSHIPS

THERE ARE a few general norms that apply to all people in an agency, and a great many that apply to specific types of social relationships. The general ones are considered first.

An over-all rule is: *"Don't lie, cheat, steal unnecessarily."* This is the same rule as applied to the public, but now it is applied as a norm for interpersonal relations. Again the same general limits apply. A great many otherwise unacceptable actions are viewed as tolerable (except to the injured party) because all are aware of the pressure that causes individuals to act in ways that are outside the Judeo-Christian ethical framework. The individual whose ethical lapses are due only to a desire for personal advantage or for "joy through crime" is viewed as a moral leper. If one lies to avoid endangering the agency or to avoid losing one's job, then the lie is necessary.

Another norm involves keeping one's promises. The rule is: *"Don't make empty promises; but when you make a promise, keep it."* This is a general application of the norm of not lying to the client. The individual must establish himself as being trustworthy. To do so he must keep his personal promises. However, he should not place himself in embarrassing situations by giving promises he cannot meet. Personal honor, in this sense, is one of the most valued qualities in a man. Word-keeping indicates "character," and helps a man to gain the reputation of being "responsible"—an indispensable quality for mobility to "business-oriented" positions.

The demand for word-keeping is nevertheless not so stringent as may first appear. If there is a choice between keeping one's word to a client or a superior, and keeping it to a peer or an inferior, the choice is always made in favor of the former. This is excusable if the promise was made in good faith and if the conflict in promises was unavoidable. Again, all parties recognize the pressures involved.

The moral leper makes indiscriminate promises that he has

no intention of fulfilling or that he fails to fulfill simply because of inconvenience.

A third general rule involves one's private life. The agency makes no demands on the individual's private morals, ethics, or character so long as they do not impinge upon the conduct of business or on agency-client relationships. An individual can be a homosexual, a lecher, a drunk, or a psychopath just so long as he is discreet. He should not display his vices in the office, nor should he get his name in the papers. The client, in short, should think of an agency man as a pillar of the community unless, of course, the client is a lecher or a semialcoholic himself. In that case, the agency man may assist the client in assuaging his vicious needs. But in every case, the obligation is to keep one's ill-fame out of the newspapers.

As for their personal standards of judgment, agency men appear to be tolerant of others' idiosyncrasies as long as they are not obtrusive or threatening. One does not impose one's personal taste on others.

A final rule, more a job requirement than an ethical norm, is: *"Never lose your temper, no matter what the provocation."* Losing one's temper causes the individual to say things, or expose things, that are best left unsaid or unexposed. Personal control is a means of avoiding "spilling the beans." And spilling the beans is one of the most serious violations of agency norms. Being a vicious gossip, in or not in anger, is almost automatic grounds for firing.

ETHICS FOR BOSSES WITH RESPECT TO THEIR SUBORDINATES

A BOSS is expected to give credit to juniors for work they have done. He should not "hog" the glory. It is assumed that, since most work in an agency is collective work, it is not necessary for one man to have all the credit. Moreover, since the boss recruits, hires, trains, and supervises the work of his subordinates, credit for a subordinate's outstanding work automatically belongs to the boss. Since this is true, the boss gets the credit, even if he graciously renounces it in favor of his subordinates. The boss who "hogs the glory," then, takes the credit he would get anyway, but takes it by denying it unnecessarily to others. He gets the reputation of being a moral leper, and subordinates seek to transfer from his jurisdiction, if necessary to another agency. They may even attempt to keep their ideas secret, announcing them only in public meetings in which their bosses' peers or superiors (including representatives of the client) are present.

Similarly, a boss is expected to take the blame for a subordinate's mistake, even though the boss is not responsible for the mistake. He is viewed as responsible for hiring the miscreant and for supervising his work. If a mistake reaches that point where it can be publicly called a mistake, the boss has failed. If he is a "man," he will take the blame in public and settle with the subordinate in private.

This norm is again limited by the norm of pressure. If the boss is endangered personally by the mistake of the subordinate, it is "understood" when he allows the subordinate to take the blame. If he does so when there is no pressure, he approaches moral leprosy. When he allows a subordinate to take the blame gratuitously for his, i.e. the boss's, mistakes, he is a moral leper.

Additionally, the boss is expected to try to get higher salaries and stock for his subordinates and to fight for them when they are criticized by the personnel of other departments. He does so because his subordinates are extensions of himself. He asserts his self-esteem by fighting for his "children." Not infrequently, though, the boss may think that there is a "fixed pool" of money available for raises in his department, or a fixed amount of stock available for such disposition. He can thus conceive of himself in competition with his subordinates. To get a larger share for himself, he denies benefits to his subordinates. The latter, if they find out, will conceive of the boss as a leper, and act accordingly.

A boss is allowed the pleasure of inventing "exercises" for his subordinates—hard, senseless work that keeps them on their toes and reminds them who is boss. However, this right is limited. He should rotate his "favors" among subordinates. Picking on one man is regarded as a sign of weakness rather than strength. Causing a subordinate to break down because of unnecessary exercises or pressure is a stigma of moral leprosy. In short, no matter how great the pressures placed on him, the boss is obligated not to increase the pressures on his subordinates just to make someone suffer as much as he does. This norm is more honored in its breach than in its acceptance. The boss who does honor the norm is viewed somewhat as a saint in Ivy League clothes.

ETHICS FOR SUBORDINATES WITH RESPECT TO THEIR BOSSES

THE ETHICAL NORMS for this situation come close to being work rules. Since the boss has means of enforcing the norms, the individual may comply simply in recognition of the power differentials involved. Yet advertising men do recognize some as ethical norms. These will be listed briefly:

1. Never denigrate your boss, even in situations where he has no chance of hearing about it.

2. Never take credit for your own work unless the boss has publicly acknowledged your contribution. After he has done so, one should modestly acknowledge the help, encouragement, and contribution of the boss.

3. Take the blame for the boss's mistakes if it won't get you fired.

4. Never go over the boss's head; don't squeal on him to *his* boss.

5. If you know that your boss disagrees with his boss or with the client but is afraid to express his disagreement, express the boss's arguments for him, even if you don't agree, so long as it doesn't get you fired.

6. Always show deference and respect for the boss in public situations.

7. In short, loyalty, deference, trustworthiness, reliability, are all indispensable characteristics of the good subordinate.

ETHICAL NORMS APPLYING TO
PEER RELATIONSHIPS

THE NORMS that especially govern relationships between equals, or between individuals who are not in a supersubordinate relationship, are essentially norms that define and regulate unfair competition.

The paramount norm of this order is: *Don't squeal to the boss about the derelictions of your peers."* The individual who squeals is a moral leper not only to the injured party but also to the boss and to anyone who discovers the tale-bearing. The reason is obvious. An individual who squeals against a peer is capable of squealing against a boss to the boss's boss, or against the agency to the client. Squealing is thus evidence of untrustworthiness. It also is indicative of an inability to handle oneself in competition. Only the man who is incapable of taking care of himself "runs to Papa." Squealing thus indicates lack of manliness, lack of toughness, and lack of nerve.

The boss may encourage a subordinate who squeals to him. But if the subordinate does squeal, the boss may punish the party squealed against and distrust the "spy" who squealed. He is likely to inform the victim of the name of the informer and perhaps encourage the growth of counterinforming. The boss who encourages subordinates to inform against one another is also considered by them to be morally leprous.

The norm against squealing is likely to cause a great deal of personal conflict and anxiety on the part of an individual who is aware of malfeasances committed by his peers. If he squeals, he is considered untrustworthy; if he does not, the malefactor can endanger himself, the account, the boss, or the agency. The individual must learn techniques whereby malfeasances can be brought to light without resort to squealing. He must arrange for the boss to discover the "crime" before it is too late. In the case of "too-lateness," he must pretend not to have known about the crime because, had he known, he could have helped prevent it at the cost of acquiring the stigma of being an informer.

The ethical norms against squealing and against losing

one's temper substantially limit the techniques of interpersonal competition and rivalry. As we have indicated, advertising men are frequently in serious competition with all whom they work for and with, even though they are dependent upon those with whom they compete. The forms of competition are further circumscribed by norms against squealing, loss of temper, and direct appeals to authority. The solution to this problem is simple in theory and difficult in practice.

If there is to be competition, rivalry, and conflict between individuals, the norms "require" that all competitive activity be expressed in terms of the objective, stated, and public business of the agency. In appearance, this means doing a better job than a peer, or attempting to prove on objective grounds that the job one does is so good that all other jobs must, by implication, suffer in comparison.

One waits for or arranges an issue where one is diametrically opposed to the rival on objective grounds. One marshals one's facts, arguments, and supporters to one's offense or defense after the rival has committed himself irretrievably to his position. One impersonally, objectively, and without anger demolishes the rival's arguments and does this so conclusively that his nerve fails. If he concedes defeat, loses his temper, or is publicly embarrassed over a major issue, he may be forced to resign. The ultimate argument is that the rival's policy would result in the loss of an account, the inability to secure business, or the embarrassment of the agency before the client.

If the rival adopts this same line of attack against an individual, the latter can respond in a number of ways. He can refuse to become committed irretrievably to a position, and thus remain inaccessible to attack. Or he can have his defense, his arguments and facts, all prepared to meet the issue whenever it is pressed. The "likable fellow" attempts to avoid attack by never placing himself irretrievably in any position. He may succeed for a long time. He may take a position only after a stronger person, a "tough realist," has affirmed the same position. No individual can avoid taking a position indefinitely. This is the weakness of the "likable fellow." By not taking a position, he can be accused of neglecting his responsibility to the client. The client demands the best policy for his brand; having no policy is having a bad policy. If the "likable fellow" hides behind a "tough realist," he condemns himself to a subaltern's role. What is more, he is likely to be considered as not quite a "man," someone whom one does not have to reckon with. Moreover, a "tough realist" can reverse himself suddenly, leaving the sycophant high and dry. When this happens, the "likable fellow" may find himself committed to an irretrievable issue.

The "tough realist" is a man who can recognize when an irretrievable issue is being raised, can foresee when to decline or accept the issue, and can carry his position through to a successful conclusion when he does accept such an issue. Fortunately for all parties concerned, such irretrievable issues do not occur frequently, and when they do they can often be avoided.

Another ethical norm governs the ethics or perhaps the aesthetics of defeat. If one has been publicly humiliated, has lost one's nerve, or has been revealed as a "dangerous" person in a semipublic situation, one is done for. A person knows he is done for when other agency personnel begin to avoid him, when subordinates become less deferential or even argumentative or insolent, when peers begin to disagree with his most innocuous, agreeable statements, and when bosses begin to give him a continuous series of exercises or no work at all. The ethical thing to do in such a situation is to look for another job or, if necessary, to resign. By hanging around after having outlived one's usefulness, one reminds others that it could happen to them. One tempts others to self-destructive sympathy. One evokes guilt in the party who "necessarily" caused the defeat. One becomes an open sore in an organization that needs healthy defenses to stand the day-to-day pressures of work. Agencies are likely to give such a person plenty of time to find another job so that he does not have to appear unemployed while looking for it. What is unethical in this situation is to force one's boss to fire one. When one does so, one forces the boss personally and falsely to bear the guilt of firing a man, when that act is actually due to the remorseless operation of the system.

One final ethical norm regulates the relationship between

peers. This is related to the stealing of ideas. Ideas, plans, proposals, slogans, strategies are the basis of an agency's existence. Being fruitful is a major way toward success in an agency. It might, therefore, be expected that stealing ideas would be a major violation of advertising ethics. Yet stealing ideas is at most a minor vice. If an idea has been successfully stolen, it has been useful to boss, agency, or client. No one complains about a useless idea that has been stolen. Thus the boss, agency, executive, or client that accepts a stolen idea is pleased (at the moment of acceptance) with the idea. He is less concerned with the origins of the idea than with its utility. Moreover, the thief of an idea, to be successful, must first be able to "sell" the idea. The idea becomes an objective reality when it is "sold." Thus, originating an idea is less important than selling it. The originator is to be pitied only if he allowed someone else to steal and sell his idea. The thief is not to be blamed.

The originator may have a sense of personal injury toward the thief, but the sense of loss is not transferred to higher levels so long as the agency gets credit for serving the client. When a man gets the reputation of stealing all his ideas, either from peers or outsiders, he is *not* considered to be a moral leper so long as he steals "good" ideas and sells them successfully. But he earns disapprobation on other grounds. A man who is forced to steal ideas obviously cannot create them. Stealing ideas thus is proof of lack of creativity, talent, and imagination. Such an evaluation of a man is made not on ethical grounds but on grounds of lack of ability. It is made primarily by his peers and not by his superiors. Superiors are concerned with results. A successful idea is a successful idea no matter where it originates, and one should perhaps not inquire too closely concerning sources.

CONCLUSION

THE IMAGE we present of advertising is not a pleasant one. In some sense we have overdrawn the picture. Certainly the norms of not losing one's temper, and of competing in terms of public, objective, and functional purpose, mean that the public life of the agency does not appear unhealthy. Moreover, the relatively quick resignation of the "open sores" keeps the "unhealthy-looking" man from beclouding the sunny, optimistic, and constructive atmosphere of the agency.

In addition, it is difficult to be overly critical of advertising because it is not so very different from most areas of upper-middle-class life. We have noted that advertising is different from other "executive suite" life only insofar as it distills and concentrates the essence of the executive suite. Advertising pays the same material rewards that are central to the American dream. The rewards are greater than can usually be found in other businesses and are available to more individuals. It is perhaps only just that the risks—personal, professional, and psychological—are greater in advertising than in most other professions. If one wants to play for big stakes, one must be prepared to suffer big losses.

Moreover, simply because of the pressures, difficulties, and irrationalities that are central to its structure, advertising recruits, selects, and rewards those individuals who are psychologically attuned to its environment. In addition to material rewards, it offers deep-seated psychological rewards, a feeling of narcissistic well-being, to those who can meet the demands imposed on them by the nature of the work itself. It is unfortunate that many men discover only after having devoted half a career to advertising that they are not equipped to work in the field. This belated discovery occurs only because the demands and pressure placed upon a man increase with length of service and with responsibility. Moreover, failure in advertising is often more final than in other professions.

One way to evaluate advertising as a career or a profession is to ask the questions, "Would you recommend advertising as a career to the son of a dear friend?" and, "Under what conditions would you recommend it?"

The answer that this author would make constitutes his summary of this essay. If the son has genuine talent or creative ability in any field, advertising is the last place for him to be. A truly autonomous, creative person will find the pressures of committee politics and decision-making destructive of his creative talent. If he accepts his new assignments, he must experience guilt for having betrayed his original talent.

If the friend's son is kind, gentle, ethical, or religious, and believes in spontaneous social relationships, advertising would be an incompatible profession. Advertising requires strong defenses, toughness, nerve, the willingness to exploit oneself and others. Our young man might crack under the pressure or, worse, develop these characteristics necessary for occupational survival.

There are individuals for whom one could recommend advertising as a profession. If a young man had no great creative talent but was a good technician in an applicable field, he might be a prospect one could recommend. If he was fairly bright but had no talents, he might also be a prospect. In addition, he would need a healthy constitution, "nerve" but no nerves, and the capacity for hard but not necessarily meaningful work. He would have to have the capacity for handling himself, tact, and the ability to enjoy superficial social relationships. He should be something of a show-off who could control the need to show off and, in doing so, be able to enjoy showing off to himself.

If he had all these qualities, and if monetary success or the sense of power was a sufficient motivation for his actions, he could be a successful and, perhaps, well-adjusted advertising man.

Obviously, advertising does attract the kind of men it needs to do a reasonably effective job of selling its clients' wares. In doing so, advertising as an industry fulfills the requirements placed upon it by other segments of the economy. Because it does so, it is difficult to say that advertising is better or worse than the society for which it is a cynosure. If advertising is to be condemned, much of our society is also to be condemned.

But as a place of work advertising leaves much to be desired. All work, but especially advertising, demands that the worker give much of his total personality, his total self, to the job. The very creative sources of a man are involved in what he gives to others through his work and what he receives from others by virtue of his work. The quality of one's work shapes, channels, and gives expression to one's creative energy. If the job demands the ability to exploit and manipulate others, both in personal and in impersonal relationships, the very self that provides the basic energy for these actions must of necessity be corroded by these actions. If one attempts to build walls against one's own exploitation and against attempted exploitation by others, a great deal of one's psychic energy is invested merely in self-protection. It is no wonder that the field is populated by would-be artists, novelists, scholars, and poets who rarely manage to fulfill the promise that gave meaning to their youth.

It is perhaps not demanding too much to ask of people to give to their work that which in themselves they value most highly—in abstract terms, love, creativity, authenticity. But these demands cannot be made of the vast majority of employed persons in our essentially materialistic society, since the demands made by their work are somewhat less than individuals at their best can give and, more often, are somewhat perverted versions of what individuals at their best have to offer.

Advertising simply accepts the world as it is, and then makes it even more so.

PART II

✻

The Structure of Nonprofit Work

ADVERTISING VERSUS NONPROFIT WORK

THE DISCUSSION of advertising suggests a number of central characteristics of the advertising agency and of work in an agency. To summarize, some of these characteristics are:

1. Labor intensiveness and capital extensiveness.
2. The possibilities of great opportunities for achieving rapid advancement, high incomes, and wealth, and
3. The possibility of sudden unemployment, with the risk of total failure after the initial achievement of high levels of income and occupational mobility.
4. The inability of the advertising per se to prove in any *specific, objective way* the contribution of its efforts to the success of the client, and
5. The parallel inability of an individual in the agency to prove his contribution to the agency, despite the fact that advertising in total is presumed by both agency and client to have tremendous effects on sales of a brand.
6. From an economic point of view this is all that is necessary; from a moral point of view, the ideological failure has resulted in irony, cynicism, self-mockery, and attitudes of estrangement among agency personnel which color their whole way of life.

These characteristics can serve as a paradigm for the analysis of nonprofit agencies and work. Of course, it must be recognized that advertising work is not typical of all profit-making work. Rather it represents the extreme end of a hypothetical scale, the opposite pole being highly altruistic, nonprofit, low-paying work. That opposite might be the work in a Trappist monastery or perhaps the work of a forest ranger.

Most other profit-making agencies appear to be not as

profitable as advertising, not as frenetic; they are ideologically more respectable and not so destructive of simple ideals; and the results they produce are more measurable than those of advertising. But almost all share to some extent the basic characteristics of advertising. Thus advertising can be viewed as the essence of the more commercial aspects of American civilization.

Nonprofit work in government, in foundations and universities, in public and private social welfare agencies, among others, displays vast differences in the administrative, financial, and technological spheres of these agencies as well as in their manifest tasks; and it is difficult to generalize about them collectively. In the discussions that follow, we will deal separately with differing types of organization.

THE IDEOLOGIES OF
NONPROFIT AGENCIES

ALL NONPROFIT ORGANIZATIONS have one thing in common, as opposed to advertising, and that is an ideology. The ideologies of nonprofit organizations stress higher purposes, nobler ends, and ultimate ideals. These include the saving or preserving of the lives of men, their souls or their psyches, their culture, their knowledge, and their potentialities.

Moreover, these purposes are legitimized and sanctified by age-old traditions, beliefs, and dogmas. The disinterested search for knowledge and truth was a relatively early ideology, originating in the Athenian academy and supported by medieval scholasticism and Renaissance humanism. The pursuit of science is only a modification of these older ideals, although in its origins in the fourteenth century it seemed to be radical.

Many of the professions which are supported by nonprofit organizations are relatively new. Social work, for instance, a profession requiring specific, technical graduate training is only a twentieth-century phenomenon. As such, it faces the problem of every profession, of justifying its special claims for the prestige, financial support, and influence formerly claimed by those older occupations and professions which occupied the areas the new profession now claims itself peculiarly qualified to monopolize. At the same time, some social workers must struggle with other new professions—psychiatry, public administration, psychology, "education," and "the law"—which would also occupy these areas. But regardless of these battles among the virtuous, social work can justify its higher purpose through its special function of helping the deprived, the handicapped, the needy, the helpless, and can, if necessary, find legitimacy back at least as far as the English poor laws or, if necessary, the activities of the medieval regular orders and the injunctions in the New and Old Testaments to "help and love thy neighbor."

Social work is only an example, demonstrating the higher ideological purposes that support nonprofit work. Once we understand the source of legitimacy of these institutions, it is perhaps easier to understand the failure of advertising and business to develop an ideology that enables its practitioners to accept their own practices without qualms, guilt, irony, or defensiveness. Purely economic activity—profit-making, wealth-getting—are clearly on the defensive in our society. The businessman is constantly forced to justify himself, despite the Protestant ethic, the ideology of laissez-faire and the past propaganda of the National Association of Manufacturers, the U.S. Chamber of Commerce, the Rotary clubs, and the countless booster clubs of Main Street. These operate more to reassure the businessmen than to convince the public. At least businessmen are their own best audiences. In a society created and sustained by business it is a supreme irony that the businessman is continually forced to justify his activity by never relaxing in his attempts to brainwash himself as well as others.

Thus, in emphasizing the nobility of their ultimate goals, the high-minded professions cannot help but (and rarely try to) denigrate the goals of the "vulgar" businessman who traffics in the muck and mire of ordinary daily existence.

By and large the high-minded have been more successful

than the businessman in diffusing their values, even to the point were they instill guilt, defensiveness, and ideological insecurity in the businessman. In a sense this is inevitable. The skills of the high-minded have always been in writing, speaking, teaching, and argumentation. Business has depended on *doing*. When it has become aware of the need for counterpropaganda, it has been forced to employ intellectuals, and they have always been available in large numbers for such profitable employment.

These ideologies of service and high ideals are more than ideologies or defenses of one social group or profession against the ideological assaults of other groups. They constitute the basis of the self-definition of the group and of the development of personal and occupational pride, security, and motivation of its members. The strength and tradition of the ideological legitimacy of the high-minded professions give them a peculiar source of inner security. They can look down their noses at the merely human; they can justify their lower salaries, find psychological compensation for their lack of material success, and at the same time express their resentment at the lack of material rewards. They can develop some of the ideologies of an aristocracy in feeling that "mere" businessmen are a lower species of animal and are therefore not entitled to the protection of the ethical norms which allegedly govern relations among the high-minded. Thus businessmen are fair game for the high-minded. They can be exploited, lied to, conned, and made to feel inadequate. They are denigrated, satirized, and "exposed" in articles, books, and classroom lectures. But as sources of finances, contracts, and consultancies they are given pseudodeference and formal prestige. Their economic power is recognized, and the extreme critics of business are often both obsequious in their presence and proud of the ability to appear obsequious and fool the "idiot businessman." The attitude of moral superiority that high-minded ideologies provide to their practitioners, moreover, not only serves to vindicate the lower pay they receive, but sustains the role itself. That is, nonprofit occupations are assumed to be more virtuous and legitimate per se. The official can point to his position, his title, his rank, and claim the prestige benefits implicit in the ideology and history of his profession and role, without having to validate that claim personally. A professor is a better man than a businessman more by virtue of his occupation than by virtue of anything he himself does professionally to advance science, art, or humanity. He can if he wishes rest on historical laurels and hope that no one finds him out. His claims to moral superiority can thus be very thin, but he, like the aristocratic, rests on his pedigree. The businessman, and especially the advertising man, because his legitimacy is based less on ideological function and more upon ability to deliver a specific product which is reputed to have cash value, can properly raise the question "What have you done for me lately?"

THE ORGANIZATION OF NONPROFIT WORK

THE SPECIAL CHARACTERISTICS of an occupation or profession are in part a function of its organizational structure and economic basis. Since nonprofit organizations have a wide variety of organizational forms it is necessary to describe some of these specific forms, especially as they affect the nature and flow of the work they do.

Government organizations increasingly tend to be bureaucratized. They have rigidly defined job descriptions, which are hierarchichal in nature and specialized, and which operate through established routines and paper work. At the lower levels the flow of work is orderly (if not always meaningful), paced, and undemanding. In fact, the bureaucracies' very rigid and precise legal definitions of roles make it possible for the lower-ranking bureaucrat to resist the work demands of his superiors. These demands do not, in and of themselves, constitute stimuli to going beyond the limited productivity of routine. Individuals experienced in private business are continually irritated by lower-level civil servants who are experts in legal arguments to justify ways of delaying or not doing work. The "civil servant" lacks authority to do the job; he insists upon proper paper work and procedures, and he insists on following proper channels if doing so delays the work. The organizational structure is viewed as a means of delaying work and of protecting the civil servant from its demands. In business the organization is viewed as the vehicle for getting work done. There are relatively few pressures in the civil service for sustained and intensive work, and there are no short and demanding deadlines. Only at the times of the annual report and of the submission of the departmental budget and its defense is there an air of crisis in the public bureaucracies. At these times all hands are commandeered to gather and assemble and present the data necessary to justify past budgets and support future ones. At these times all hands are willing to pitch in and to work enthusiastically day and night (even at times without overtime pay). Morale and a sense of excitement run high, and members of the organization are generally surprised at the amount and caliber of work they are capable of doing. But such exercises are of relatively short duration (less than a month) and occur only once or twice a year. In the interim, work slackens off to an easy pace which the individuals enjoy and which allows them to complain of lack of involvement in the work.

At the higher levels of the civil service bureaucracies these descriptions do not apply. Because the upper ranks of bureaucracies are necessarily political, the work in these ranks is just as demanding as in the advertising agency even though the bureaucrat is hemmed in by rules and procedures and is limited in the rewards he receives. The politics are not the open politics of political parties but rather the closed politics of "the corridors of power," as C. P. Snow has described them. Involved in these closed politics is the maintenance of friendly relations with other departments, superiors, political officers in the legislative and executive branches, and relevant and influential publics and the press. These politics involve the development of plans for the operation of one's agency, for the formulation of new policies relevant to one's departmental mission, and for securing support and pressure to actualize these plans. They involve fighting the plans and designs of competitive departments and the hostile pressures that would limit or narrow the jurisdiction of one's own department. They necessarily involve either attempts to maximize the efficiency of one's department or the avoidance of criticism for inefficiency. The middle- and high-ranking bureaucrat is thus an important, busy person who has and uses a great deal of disciplined energy. His personal motives go hand in hand with the ideology of service. At times, however, he sees a disjunction between this personality and ideology, because tactics and political necessities force him to limit his ideals in order to survive the bureaucratic wars. An ideology of "acceptance of reality" always implies that reality is unpleasant.

THE STRUCTURE OF ACADEMIC WORK

THE COLLEGE PROFESSOR is in a position entirely different from that of the bureaucrat, despite the fact that the universities are increasingly being bureaucratized. The medieval university was a collection of colleges, each college being a self-governing body of guild members whose work was the accumulation and dissemination of knowledge. The college was self-governing, with the rector or the master of the college being elected by its members. Church-operated schools, however, were bureaucratic in structure. In the United States the tradition of faculty-operated schools (at least in the determination of academic policy) coexisted with a policy of schools run by lay boards selected from the outstanding laity of the congregation, who in early American history ran the American college or university.

In the state and municipal colleges and universities, administrative officers appointed by lay boards were responsible to the legislative bodies but made policy by means of uneasy cooperation with faculty committees. With the growth of mass higher education after World War II, the role of the faculty has been continually reduced. Trained "educators" and educational administrators increasingly man the administrative machinery and by nature of their inside position reduce the role of the faculty to that of either a rubber stamp or an intransigent obstacle. By and large the faculty accedes willingly to the demands of the professional administrator since in surrendering its rights to formulate and make policy, it frees itself from time-consuming "petty" committee and administrative work, which is regarded as an interference with the higher puposes of the faculty.

The professorial position is unique in American society, because the professor's work load is deliberately designed to allow him a maximum of free time. Even a severe teaching load of fifteen hours a week, allowing for preparation, committee work, and counseling of students, would, by standards of industry, be a light load for a middle- or high-ranking executive, especially when intersessions and summer vacations are considered. However, a load of fifteen hours a week is considered intolerable by most academicians today, and no reputable university can attract a competent staff with such a work load regardless of pay. Twelve-hour loads are currently considered to be undesirable, with a nine-hour load assumed to be the norm. The great graduate schools increasingly attract top faculty by paying larger and larger salaries: $20,000 to $25,000 a year is not unusual; salaries of $45,000 to $100,000 are conspicuous public relations devices used to advertise the school by virtue both of the salaries involved and of the public relations value of the names so attracted. To be sure, the contribution and skill of the personnel so attracted may be as great or greater than that of businessmen and of professionals in such fields as law or medicine who command higher salaries. In addition to such salaries the teaching load is often held down to three to six hours a week.

The relatively light teaching loads which professors are offered and the still lighter ones that they demand are functions of the intrinsic nature of the professorial role. A teaching position is, in effect, a benefice, which imposes on its occupant a minimum of routine duties and pressures and offers a maximum of free time, during which he is expected to write and conduct research. Thus academic work consists of three sets of demands: (1) teaching, (2) scholarly writing and research and (3) administrative services to the school.

Teaching can be one of the most satisfying of any occupation. Assuming that the professor is assigned courses related to his interests and specialty, he has the opportunity to read along the lines of his interests and to present his thoughts to an audience which ranges from uninterested but dutiful clods to a few students who can be inspired by the possibilities inherent in any advanced field. No field is dull in itself; there are only dull teachers and dull students. The teacher, if he finds he can attain or maintain his interests in a field, will find interested students who are transported by either the subject matter or the enthusiasm of the teacher. A dull teacher produces dull students, and not vice versa.

Teaching, unlike research, is a performing art. The enthusiastic teacher receives stimulation from the response of his audience and can be exhilarated by his own response to his performance and by the response of his students. If his personality is histrionic he can find the teaching situation especially pleasurable. He can, if he is overexhilarated by it, become primarily an actor, arranging his materials to produce special effects regardless of the accuracy of his presentation. Every major university has these histrionic lecturers; their courses are a school tradition. They present special jokes, bizarre examples, rhetorical and vocal effects, shock treatments for the sensibilities of undergraduates, public blasphemy, and professorial superiority over the Philistine world. Most of these professorial prophets are frauds. The fact that the audience is not an audience of peers but rather of neophytes makes the fraudulence possible. The appreciation of neophytes of dramatic overcooking confirms and inflates the megalomania and histrionics of the teacher who has these tendencies.

Other aspects of teaching are equally satisfying. Because the enthusiasm and sincerity of the student communicate themselves to the professor, a serious teacher can find in the response of serious students the opportunity to relive and recreate his youth and the ideals of his youth. When this happens the professor has no need to surrender his ideals and youthful enthusiasm to the "realities of life," a term which in our society means accommodation to cynicism and defeat, to a sense of powerlessness in the face of a hostile and intractable world. More readily than the followers of any other occupation, professors can, if they wish, preserve their youthful enthusiasm, but only if they are responsive to the best in their students. They owe as much to their students as the students owe to them.

A professor, especially one in graduate education, has the opportunity of seeing his students grow in competence and maturity. Starting from a position of uninformed, enthusiastic immaturity, the student can grow intellectually until he becomes the peer of the professor. If the teacher does not find it necessary to maintain an attitude of superiority over his students, his capacity to see direct and immediate effects of his work in their achievement can produce in him profound feelings of satisfaction. In almost a generic sense, teaching contains the elements of the parent-child relationship. At its best it is sublime; but as we shall see, it can also be hell.

When teaching results in the mutual engagement of the student and teacher in the common media and discipline of the content and technique of a field, the histrionic aspects of teaching become either an irrelevancy or an obstacle. The enjoyment of work itself is all that is necessary. The truly great teachers need not be colorful, dramatic, or "interesting." They need only to be concerned with their work. Thus the great teachers in America—Veblen, Dewey, G. H. Mead, Beard, Parrington, Vivas, and Gerth—were not by and large histrionic teachers. By all standards of professional education and entertainment they were frequently dull teachers. All they had was the capacity to stimulate, excite, and develop a vast number of students whose creative work would not have been possible without the example of devotion to their respective fields provided by the teacher.

Needless to say, very few teachers are histrionic frauds, and very few are truly great teachers. The ability of average college teachers ranges from almost incoherent incompetence to dull mediocrity.

Why this is so is puzzling. Some college teachers go into teaching only because it presents opportunities for research; they are incompatible with or despise the teaching role. Others like the teaching role but feel that it takes too much time away from their research activities. By and large, however, a strong devotion to research produces a good teacher, because with a strong interest in research the teacher communicates that enthusiasm, which makes for good teaching. Perhaps it is boredom, the lack of enthusiasm for one's subject matter, that results in so much poor teaching. Despite the fact that college teaching is usually geared to the interests and specialization of the professor, many academicians are not able to sustain their interests and enthusiasm. In part this may be due to the necessity of having to repeat elementary material to classes of undergraduates while one's interests continue to grow. In part, I would venture to say, the much greater part, boredom with oneself and field sets in after a few years of teaching. The boredom reflects itself in a dependence on old notes (some college teachers are known to teach from notes that are from twenty-five to forty years old) and in an unwillingness to read new works in one's field (some teachers are unwilling to read much that has been written after they have obtained their Ph.D. or completed their first course preparations). Some rely on textbooks as their source of reading (and in so doing make dullness the input of the teaching process), and others may be constitutionally dull.

Yet with all this, "teaching" is an ideology of many college teachers and college administrators. This concern for the quality of teaching stems from the fact that more and more of the faculties of the great universities are engaged in working on foundation grants or governmental contract research. Part of a grant includes funds to pay the university for the time which the professor devotes to his research instead of to teaching. As a result, the researcher's teaching replacement is usually a graduate student or a less distinguished faculty member. (If he were more distinguished, he might have his own grant.) As a result, the university chair more and more provides more and more office space, a letterhead, and scientific respectability for academic entrepreneurs. Presidents of the most prestigious (and most heavily endowed) universities, as well as "radical" student leaders, would genuinely like to see their most distinguished faculty members actually do some teaching. They also like to see their faculty gain research grants which enhance both the financial resources and the prestige of their graduate schools.

The interest in good teaching is in part suspect. Many college administrators are themselves refugees from teaching. More important, teaching is a residual function in the university. We have indicated that teaching is a benefice designed, by the lightness of its load, to allow the scholar to write or do research. If one does not write or do research one must legitimatize oneself by emphasizing teaching or by "service to the college." It is precisely those teachers who do nothing else who talk most about the importance of teaching. These, because they lack enthusiasm and interest in their field, are generally the worst teachers. The "ideology" of teaching, however, is necessary, since without it there is no basis for self-justification. Some professors adjust to the residual functions of teaching by concentrating their efforts on the mechanics of teaching. Making and grading an examination can fill hundreds of hours of work, as can preparation of syllabi, class projects, and special techniques of group and class discussions. Teaching thus becomes an administrative operation, which can be carried on with little contact with one's subject matter. Such dutiful administration enables the teacher to complain of overwork without doing any substantive work except that of shuffling papers. It makes it possible for him not to write or do research, though that is the principal basis for his employment.

When a teacher is dull, bored, and uninterested, he cannot help but convey his fundamental attitude to his students. A few students will always be willing to be interested in the dullest teacher if they feel that such interest will raise their grade level. A few may be interested in the material despite the teacher. The majority will retreat to a defensive boredom which confirms the professor's own estimate that students are stupid and dull. A few students will be unable or barely able to conceal their hostility to those teachers who, by their attitude, make college attendance a waste of time. In total one would guess the undergraduate college experience tends to dampen more enthusiasm for learning than it evokes. In any one school, it is only a handful of dedicated and enthusiastic teachers who account for a meaningful college experience to the fortunate few who are exposed to them. Despite this, "teaching ability" is a major ground for promotion and for tenure in the school. Teaching is relatively more important in those schools which do not emphasize research. The judgment of who is a good teacher is frequently left in the hands of older professors and administrators, who, because of a longer tenure and history of boredom, are among the worst of the teachers.

Although teaching ability is a major criterion for promotion and achievement of tenure, objective measures of good teaching are hard to arrive at. Conspicuously good and conspicuously bad teachers develop reputations among the student body which become diffused to the faculty. However, a conspicuously bad teacher who is an associate or full professor or a department chairman is rarely the source of complaint because students and faculty have more respect for the position than for the man. The young instructor, the assistant professor, the teacher without tenure, or the one who is known to be out of favor is the object of complaints directed not only at his own teaching but at all bad teaching. In this sense the "quality of teaching" increases with age, rank, and tenure.

The histrionic teacher is most appreciated when teaching survey courses. The freshmen and sophomores, who are the majority of the students in these courses, find him entertaining, and the course becomes a traditional "experience" to be recalled and treasured by the old grads. The teacher with histrionic talents can attract large numbers of students into his courses, which increases the student-to-faculty ratio of the department, and thus reduces the cost of instruction for the students, and provides funds to pay the salaries of teaching assistants and fellows. In addition, to the extent that he does this he provides his department with arguments to increase the size of the staff and the level of salaries. The popular teacher of introductory courses also attracts "majors" to his department. In doing so he provides the basis for a larger staff. He is thus indispensable to his department. Some departments resolve the problem of using popular but "misleading" teachers by providing a second course, formally or informally required of all departmental majors, that is designed to disabuse the students of all the overdramatic and incorrect notions they acquired in the course that attracted them into the field.

Popularity of the teacher thus does not necessarily mean good teaching. Some teachers are discovered to be good teachers only ten or more years after an evalution of their teaching is made. It happens not infrequently that the special students of a given teacher turn out to be the outstanding scholars and teachers in their own generation. In some cases (not too infrequently) this may occur long after their teacher has been "let go" for reasons of poor teaching.

THE RESEARCH FUNCTION OF
THE PROFESSOR

ALTHOUGH TEACHING IS the manifest function of the college professor, his job is structured primarily to provide him with the opportunity to do research and to write. It is presumed that in his graduate training the professor has developed the capacity to do independent and autonomous research, and a teaching position gives him complete freedom to do almost anything he wants to: to define his own area of research and his problem and to determine the methods by which he will solve his problem. If he needs extra money to carry out his work, he will find his school, foundations, or government agencies willing to finance part of the costs of his work. All he needs then is approval for the grant, and the approval of editors and publishers to get his work published. Editors and publishers will usually rely on his peers to judge the value of his work. Thus there are few similar situations in history that are so favorable to the development of autonomy, creativity, and independence in the scholar. Certainly the classic image of the lonely artist or scholar struggling against a Philistine world does not apply to the academician. He is paid to do what he loves to do, or what he is supposed to do.

In fact, the prevailing image of the academic world is Publish or Perish. Like most stereotypes, this image is an oversimplification and a distortion, but in the great private and state universities the stereotype holds. In many of these schools department chairmen and deans distribute forms which require the professors to indicate their research and publication plans. They are also asked at other times to bring their *curricula vitae* up to date, that is, to update their bibliography and any other evidence of prestigious or honorific scholarly work. The relationship between research plans and research completed constitutes a bookkeeping check upon the individual which is used to evaluate his work in determining the granting of tenure and promotions. In the great universities the concentration of productive scholars in a few centers results in a competition in publication frequency, a pressure that far exceeds that of the requirements of department chairmen or deans.

Frequent publication becomes a personal challenge, a way to keep up with one's peers or to excel them. Failure to publish several articles in any one year and a book every few years is viewed by peers as evidence of senescence, sterility, or failure of nerve, energy, or ideas. As these become the operative standards of excellence such "failures" become a source of guilt and depressions. In these schools teachers are driven to prove, as Milton asserted and Robert Merton has "proved," that "fame is the spur . . . that last infirmity of noble mind/To scorn delights and live laborious days." The necessity to publish thus takes on an objective character. Originally an interest in publication might have been the natural exudation of creativity, of the emergence of a new idea, or the culmination of a lifelong interest; now the need to publish overcomes all restraints imposed by the ethic of "publish only when you have something to say." The current flood of publications has by no means increased creativity. It has increased only the strain on readers.

RESEARCH CONSULTING

SINCE WORLD WAR II the federal government, private industry and foundations, and local and state governments have increasingly become aware of the resources offered by the universities in the form of underemployed technical and scientific specialists. These agencies have made available to the great universities almost unlimited funds, which the universities have been eager to grab. The great universities have pioneered in setting up research bureaus and institutes which can thus demonstrate the feasibility of such expenditures. In the major universities as large a part of the staff is devoted to such commercial research as is devoted to teaching and to individual scholarly research combined. In fact, the great universities can more properly be called research factories than knowledge or teaching factories.

A new criterion of research and scholarly competence has thus been developed—the size and numbers of research contracts that an individual brings to the university, the number of staff members these contracts employ, and the individual's ability to work on contracts brought in by others.

Those who bring in no fatted research contracts but must live off others rank lower on the totem pole than the great research impresarios whose name and contacts provide a financial and prestige resource to the university. Secondary prestige goes to those who have the ability to fulfill the requirements of the contracts, even though they cannot secure them. Ultimately, fulfillment of the contract or renewal is the measure of success, especially if scholarly publication follows in addition to privately published reports.

In all this, the volume of publication—articles, essays in anthologies, books, and privately printed (at government expense) research reports—is the measure of competence. Quality is secondary. Scholarship in the university is so specialized that it is almost impossible for a man to evaluate the quality of the work of even his immediate subordinates. Moreover, high quality in specialized work is not usually recognized in any short time. The research output of our major universities in any field is so great that increasingly "computerized" data retrieval systems are necessary to ensure that the same work is not done over and over again because previous work is overlooked. The immense volume of publication is too great to be digested. The normal course of such digestion is to allow the passage of time to cause the irrelevant, sterile, or insignificant work to be forgotten and to disappear. This takes several years, up to a decade or two. In the meantime professors must be granted tenure and promotion. Thus quantity of work serves as a substitute for quality. And the able young and older men desperately strive to meet this standard. The flood of publications therefrom necessitates the major form of research evaluation, "forgetting." Scholars who come from an older and gentler tradition, which emphasized a lifetime of work devoted to a single subject or problem and the publication of a major work at the end of one's career, necessarily resent the compulsive quest for easy fame embodied by the newer standards. They must either surrender their standard or risk the chance of being overlooked.

The emphasis on publication puts the energetic scholar desperately in need of finding outlets for what he writes. As a result scholarly journals have multiplied. The subsidized reports by government departments provide a relatively low prestige outlet for evidence of work done. The vast growth of the college population in the post-World War II era has provided a major market for publications. Book publishers scour the hinterlands for authors and editors of texts, monographs, and anthologies and publish a mass of titles, in the hope that one "hit" will subsidize a host of financial failures. They stimulate and encourage overpublication and the drowning in paper that characterizes much of our civilization. The anthology or "reader," nonbook that it is, offers a new form of publication not hitherto available.

Most scholarly journals establish a standard format for publication and have a standardized "line" on what is publishable and *au courant*. They usually reflect the highest standards of academic correctness, the established orthodoxy of a field. The anthology or reader, because its editors are more randomly selected, will publish everything, good and bad, from a variety of editorial viewpoints (orthodox and heterodox). It thus allows for greater variety and novelty of work than does the journal. The average anthology thus is more readable, more interesting, and contains better and more original work than the official journal in its field.

Although all these developments present a flood of print resulting from the necessity of publishing or perishing, the most prolific sources of such publications, as we have indicated, are the academic departments and research factories of the great public and private universities. These represent only a small part of the total teaching (but not research) staffs of American colleges and universities. For the vast majority of these the dictum "publish or perish" does not apply and never has applied. In fact, in the vast majority of American institutions of higher learning, output is restricted by conventional agreements that, if known, would be the envy of any factory worker. These conventions include that of spending a major part of one's career revising, editing, and preparing one's doctoral dissertation for publication and preparing, if possible, an article or two from the dissertation. They include that of publishing an essay or an article infrequently and, if one is ambitious, a textbook toward the end of one's career. And, as in the informal work group in industry, the productive scholar is sanctioned and penalized for being a rate buster. By conducting research, writing, and publishing he devalues the others in his department who do not do so. Here the ideology of teaching and service are important. For the scholar who is productive, it is assumed, must necessarily be neglecting teaching, counseling of students, and university service in order to write and do research. He must be throwing the load for these more important functions on his colleagues, who because of their sense of responsibility do not have time for writing. To equalize the load, the productive scholar will be saddled with additional teaching and administrative duties so that he cannot exceed his quota. He will be lectured and bullied in other ways. Most will be forced to accept these informal conventions. A few will remain productive regardless of the pressures, and a large number will leave, hoping to be hired eventually by a great university that respects quantity of output, if nothing more.

ACADEMIC ADMINISTRATION

ADMINISTRATIVE CHORES are the third major aspect of the professorial role. They have an objective and a subjective meaning. Objectively, administration is necessary. Students have to be advised, curricula developed, staffs hired, promoted, and granted tenure, departmental exams given and graded. The department must establish cooperative and competitive relations with other departments, including the counseling of students to take "required" courses, thus dividing up of enrollments and achieving its "fair" share of new positions, courses, and classrooms. It also assists in the governing of the university in such bodies as university senates, councils, and interdepartmental committees. University government and administration involve advising and cooperating and bargaining with deans who usually have veto rights over policies and procedures proposed by the faculty, and who usually have control over the agenda of university-wide and interdepartment committees.

All the above involves attendance at department and interdepartment committee meetings. Qualification for such committees is usually based on rank and tenure, with the "plums" going to associate and full professors with tenure. An individual will serve on two to seven or eight committees, some of which meet infrequently, while others will meet as often as once a week. During some periods of the school year—at the beginning of the term when the advising of students takes place and at the end of the year when graduate students are given departmental examinations—the major part of the week is filled with administrative or service chores. In addition, if the faculty member is oriented in this direction he can make a major career out of writing committee reports and following through on the business of these committees.

For most faculty members there is a vast disdain for involvement in faculty business. It takes time away from reading, teaching, writing, and research. It is viewed as an imposition. As a result the departmental chairman and deans have increasingly centralized administration in their own hands, causing resentments among faculty members who feel that the rights they neglect are denied.

A substantial minority of professors gravitate toward administrative work. In some cases this may be due to a sense of responsibility to one's department. Administrative work must be done; and in view of the flight from administration by a majority of the staff, a responsible individual will often saddle himself with the job of department chairman even though it cuts into the time he has available for research and writing. If this is his motive, he will usually find the time to do his research and writing anyway. Others will lean to administration because it is a legitimate means of avoiding research and writing. Independent research and writing require total autonomy and independence on the part of the creator, with little or no direct supervision, and a professor may well discover that he is unable to work without a routine or external rhythm imposed upon him by others. If the professor discovers this after he has committed himself to an academic career, he will be forced to find some form of external rhythm.

Academic administration is one such form. By attending meetings, involving oneself in administration procedure, and preparing reports with definite deadlines under prescribed procedures, he is able to function in an approved way.

Involvement in administration also allows the alienated academician to feel that he is doing something "real." He is making decisions, formulating policies, and carrying them out. He is not living in a world of books and students but in a world where things get done. This, in part, is an illusion. Much of academic administration involves revisions of procedures that have worked with a modicum of efficiency in the past and will continue to operate if unrevised. There is little need to hurry and change things. Decisions can be postponed, deadlines can be extended, and reports can be sent back to committee *ad infinitum,* expecially if they displease the deans. The university does not have the competitive drive of a business that forces the administrator to make sharp, definite decisions within a given time span. Thus, while believing that he is a tough, practical realist, the academic administrator can make an autonomous game of administration.

At the same time, commitment to academic administration allows the professor to live within the cocoon of the university. He can restrict his audience and his mental horizon to the internal politics and practices of the university. He can become a living repository of its rules, procedures, history, and precedents. In doing so he becomes a living embodiment of the university. He is swallowed up by it.

Finally, service to the university via administration constitutes a claim upon it for tenure and promotions. Such a claim becomes especially significant in the absence of other claims. Needless to say, in rewarding such claims the administration ensures that valuable work will be done. However, the administratively oriented academician will tend to be more patient and persistent than others in sweating out promotions, especially since he has fewer qualifications for going elsewhere when promotions are not available. Over time, such loyal, devoted servants of the university acquire seniority and authority and, if not restrained, are likely to define the image of the ideal academic man in terms of their own characteristics. If this happens, the university is likely to be overadministered and undertaught, and scholarships will be viewed as a dereliction of duty.

ADVANCEMENT AND TENURE

THE THREE AREAS, teaching, writing and research, and administrative service, constitute the framework of the academic life. They also constitute a series of alternatives among which the academician can select a major life orientation. Finally, they constitute the basis of his advancement and tenure. Securing tenure is a major event in the life of the academician, because it means that when one has tenure one has a stable base from which to operate. The young instructor or assistant professor, fresh out of graduate school with or without his Ph.D., is one of the most exploited persons in the academic world. He is given the most courses, and the least attractive, to teach even though they are frequently outside his specialty. He is given menial administrative chores, which eat up his time. He is expected to publish and write on his free time and, quite frequently, to assist the senior professors in their research and publications. He is expected to please all senior staff members despite the fact that such senior staff members may disagree violently with one another. If his department is divided into factions, he is expected either to get along with all factions or to survive by picking the winning faction. Coming out of graduate school after several years of intensive specialization, he may, in his own area, be the outstanding man on the faculty. Quite frequently he confronts senior professors whose knowledge in his area is antiquated or who have done work relevant to his own along theoretical lines directly opposed to his in areas where theoretical differences are the source of bitter conflict. Tenure is usually granted after three, five, or seven years of service, some of which can be earned in other institutions. On the first job the young academician must survive all the pitfalls and please his senior colleagues to be granted tenure. Typically the young academician will not get tenure on his first job, he may float from school to school every few years, ultimately finding a school whose need for him is as great as his need for it.

This requires moving one's family and household, breaking established friendships and routines, and acclimating oneself to new environments. It is no wonder that many academicians suffer from failure of nerve, a failure which for many of them results in taking nonacademic jobs. For others the failure brings an overwhelming desire to please those who can, by their votes, grant tenure and the surrender of the original vision which prompted the individual to enter the field. The resentment so engendered becomes part of a world view which frequently causes the academician to take ideological revenge on the nonacademic world.

Once one has received tenure, the pressure is temporarily off. One can, if one wishes, find compensation for one's suffering by hectoring and hazing those still seeking tenure and, if necessary, students. Moreover, after one has tenure, one can, by counterattacking, pay back in kind those who placed upon him the humilities and abasement necessary to the achievement of tenure. This pattern of abasement by others followed by the abasement of others accounts in part for the fact that cliques, factions, and personal and academic warfare is the normal climate of most college departments. The academic setting is quite different from that of advertising in this respect. In advertising, individuals are forced to repress hostilities, and a defeated rival is let go. Because of tenure, the walking wounded are a part of the normal furniture of the university and are free, within the boundaries of legal grounds for dismissal, to express their hostilities, resentments, envy, and rivalry. The atmosphere then of the university is more poisoned by the overt expression of dissatisfaction and hostility than any other occupational atmosphere, except perhaps that of the governmental bureaucracy. And this occurs despite the fact that no other institution in society allows its workers as much freedom to do their own work.

The contract researcher is freer from the anxieties incurred by the uncertainty of tenure, because he has merchandisable products to justify his existence. If conditions are unsatisfactory in one university, he can bargain with other schools for a new job, taking with him contracts that are attractive and profitable to these other schools. He depends not on tenure but rather on his current economic worth to his school. As a result he has more confidence in himself and regards moving as a source of opportunity rather than as a threat. In this respect he resembles more the business or advertising man than the scholar. He is likely to have contempt for the parochial scholar who is dependent on the university for his livelihood and self-esteem. He is dependent in the last analysis only on research contracts.

Once our hero has secured tenure, the same process of

anxious waiting occurs with respect to promotion. There are differences, however. The candidate for promotion has the opportunity to wait, to serve time, and thus play upon the guilt of his peers. To some degree promotions are granted on the basis of age and length of tenure simply because it is a source of embarrassment to have on the same staff a fifty-year-old assistant professor and a *wunderkind* full professor in his thirties. Some departments, however, on the basis of past hostilities are either unembarrassed or can learn to live with such embarrassments. The candidate thus can achieve some promotions after he has received tenure simply by attrition. Openings occur because of the retirement or death of seniors, and the time server tends to occupy more and more a central role in his department as he becomes a more experienced and bureaucratically knowledgeable member of the staff. Thus, in many schools, teaching (as a residual function) and administrative service, including "getting along," become more important as bases for promotion to higher positions than do scholarly activities. The latter are more important at the junior levels.

These subtle shifts in the basis for tenure and promotion account for, in part, the fact that the vast majority of schools and the vast majority of academicians surrender precisely those aspirations and motivations that cause them to enter the field.

THE STRUCTURE OF SOCIAL WORK

Social work, in many ways, is more interesting than other nonprofit work. It is a relatively new field for professional graduate training. The first graduate schools in social work began operation in the first decade of the twentieth century. Their period of greatest expansion was in the 1950s and 1960s. All told there are some sixty-five graduate schools of social work in the United States. Moreover, the areas in which social work operates are also covered by public administrators, sociologists, politicians, educators, psychologists, untrained amateurs, recreational specialists, and others. Social work has had to carve out and define a field for itself. In part this has been done by "ideologizing," by "proving" that the social worker has the special techniques to "understand," to communicate with, and to represent the poor in a world where all other professions are overladen with middle-class bias. In that social workers deal with problems of human survival among those desperately in need of help, the ideology in part consists of a peculiar self-enhancement. Social workers are morally superior to less virtuous Philistines, who work with more trivial problems.

The problems of social work are further compounded by a history of low pay. Low pay is the norm because social work has been financed out of public funds or funds reluctantly and minimally granted by private charity and philanthropy. Schools of social work have been unable to attract the best students. Moreover, in attempting to upgrade their image the schools have restricted entry into the field by insisting upon closely supervised graduate training at a time when the need for social workers has increased, if only because more and more funds are available. This dilemma is compounded by the fact that since the number of trained professionals is limited, a vast part of personnel in the field, primarily in public welfare, consists of totally untrained persons whose only qualifications are a bachelor's degree and an inability to make an occupational choice before graduation from college.

The claim to professional status by an aspiring occupation is usually supported by the claim of a special body of knowledge and techniques unique to the profession. Social workers have attempted to make such a claim but have difficulty in proving that there is anything unique about the theory, method, or practice of social work. Much of the content of social work curricula is borrowed from the many different schools of sociology, from psychology, especially clinical, Freudian, and neo-Freudian psychology, from social psychology, including group dynamics and socio- and psychodrama, small-group theory and public administration. These are frequently tossed at the student in large doses in such

short time periods that it is difficult for him to absorb anything but the words. He absorbs large doses of ideology,
however, with which he goes to confront the most difficult
problems in our world.

Social work is a unique field in that each individual
worker, like the urban schoolteacher, must in his daily work
confront his highest ideologies with the most intractable realities. The clients he wishes to help quite often will resist his
attempts to help them. They will lie, cheat, and be evasive.
They will "con" and "jive" him at times. They will refuse to
take his advice or only pretend to take it. Because of educational, cultural, and emotional deficiencies they are unable to
respond to his best efforts; and they will pretend to be stupid
if they are not. They will often regard the social worker as a
spy who investigates their private life and as an agent of the
middle-class world and its institutions who, in addition to
being stupid, is a representative of a hostile world which
devalues them. In the face of this massive resistance to his
best efforts, the social worker must work with inadequate
social, material, and personal resources. If he works for a
public agency, he will find that his job is often there to save
the municipality money by denying to indigent clients what
are obvious necessities and the few amenities which make life
bearable. He is, in fact, cast in the role of the spy, the
policeman, and the merciless judge. Even if he would like to
be helpful, the resources he can offer are limited by legal
restraints which prevent such help or restrict it to sub-
minimal levels. When social and psychological defects and
pathologies are involved, corrective action usually requires
long, expensive, personal, and highly skilled treatment or
therapy which are usually available only in specialized experimental or demonstration programs.

In addition the field worker (the caseworker) in the private
agency is subject to the decisions of lay boards whose major
qualifications consist of success in business or in marriage to
successful businessmen. Success in business, of course, includes the inheritance of money. Such lay boards usually
have a measure of self-confidence, which is based on ignorance of the specific day-to-day problems of the case

worker and of the client and on being a financial contributor. Their major form of accountability consists in writing checks. Yet the lay boards have the power to wreck a program or a career and must be listened to. Professionals thus feel they are hampered in their desire to serve their clients not only by inadequate resources but also by ignorant and misdirected supervisors and boards.

Social welfare workers in public agencies tend to feel that their bosses live in a world of paper and of legal abstractions and substitute legal and administrative formulae for knowledge of human problems, for needed resources, and for solutions to these problems.

Thus, in attempting to apply the highest ideals to the most resistant realities, the social welfare worker frequently feels trapped, frustrated, and helpless. How he responds to such situations determines his future and his character as a social welfare worker.

1. Some workers, especially those in public welfare departments, identify with the role of policeman, spy, and prosecutor. They discharge their frustration on the clients. In doing so, they attempt to detect cheating and lying, consider them a personal assault upon their professional dignity, and respond by attempting to provide the minimal aid available or to cut clients off the rolls. Such workers overidentify with the sadistic and legalistic aspects of public welfare, sometimes to the point where their supervisors are forced to warn them "to go easy" on the clients. These workers are relatively few in number.

2. A second group identifies, for personal reasons, with the clients. A worker in this group assists the client in concealing jobs and assets (or overlooks obvious concealment). He assesses a situation and interprets departmental procedures in order to gain the greatest amount of help for the client even though such procedures are clearly illegal. He risks dismissal and after much discouragement quite frequently quits. Only a few social workers can maintain this response for a long period of time, because they come into conflict with official rules.

3. Social workers, especially those in family agencies or

child guidance agencies and those serving and attached to courts, have an especially fine opportunity to play God. They can tear a family apart by convincing a spouse that divorce is the answer to his or her needs. They can recommend that a child be torn from his parent or parents and placed in a foster home. They can make recommendations to a court that determines the length of a sentence or whether a sentence is to be suspended or not. They can "close a case," which means that a client is denied welfare, and they can recommend that legal or common-law husbands be jailed for failure to provide support to wife and children.

They can exercise all the above powers with joy or with dread. They can make their decisions on the basis of much or little knowledge of a case and the individuals involved. They can rely on "theory" and clichés as a substitute for knowledge. And they are forced to make these decisions with the awareness that there is no clear way of knowing whether the consequences will show their decisions to be right or wrong. Some harden themselves to these necessities by developing a megalomanic personality. They become right, certain, and absolute, simply because they are the ones who make the decisions. They resent all influences, including inconvenient facts, that violate their sense of necessary certainty; megalomania becomes a way of life that need not handicap one professionally.

4. A fourth group, the largest number of workers in public agencies, retreat into legalism and apathy, wherein, whenever possible, paper work is substituted for personal visits, and "canned" clichés and jargon for reports of visits. This retreat involves relying on apathetic conformity as a means of staying out of trouble while not exposing oneself to the anguish of dealing with clients whom one can not help in any substantial way.

5. The quest for a work situation which allows the social worker to live his ideals results, especially for social workers in private agencies, in a high rate of job turnover. The individual worker finds his job unattractive. He feels he is overworked and underpaid; his supervisors are stupid, sadistic Philistines or charlatans; the resources to do the job are in-

adequate; and his is subject to nonprofessional interference which makes it impossible to do the job he would like to do. He emphasizes his professionalism as a defense against boards and untrained or competitive occupations which impinge upon his work. His moving from job to job is an endless quest for a social situation which allows him to reconcile his ideology with the realities of work. He is rarely successful. The social worker can escape from the treadmill of fruitless job changing by adapting some of the forms of adjustment already mentioned or by some still to be mentioned.

6. One of the common modes of escape is to discover an agency in which high-quality, specialized work is done for research or experimental purposes. Intensive and long-range treatment or therapy is given to a few specialized cases at a cost that is so high in money and manpower that it can only be justified by research and experimental rationales. The social worker, if he is fortunate enough to locate such a work situation, is able to defend his professional status, but his ideological status may suffer. He realizes that the cost of doing high-quality work makes it impossible to do that work where it needs to be done. The conflict between a professional ideology and a "humanistic" ideology thus becomes the source of much personal and group self-examination. Intellectual and ideological differences are common between, on the one hand, academic and specialized social workers who are oriented to specific problems that require intensive, experimental, and costly research, and, on the other, neighborhood settlement workers who see a vast host of problems and needs that are unmet because professionals invest vast resources in a few cases.

7. A similar pattern of response is to be found in specializing in high-prestige areas of social work like psychiatric social work, group therapy, individual counseling, and perhaps marital counseling. The virtue of such specialization is not only that it provides prestige for the social worker within his profession, but also that these types of practice allow the social worker to develop a clientele with a middle- and upper-middle-class social and economic status. Since the problems

confronting these clients are frequently not so severe as those of lower-class clients, the possibility of helping to resolve them is easier. Moreover, expertise in these specialized types of practice at times allows the social worker to go into practice for himself or, as an associate, in a private clinic together with psychiatrists or psychologists. In doing so he escapes or feels he escapes, the problems of being smothered by a vast bureaucratic agency.

8. A special form of escape through higher specialization occurs when he becomes an academician or full-time social-work researcher. When this happens, he becomes subject to all the structural and situational characteristics of the academic world, as previously discussed. In addition, professorial social work as a discipline usually has low prestige within the academic world because it is, in most schools, a "johnny-come-lately" field without a secure academic tradition of its own.

As an academician, the social worker can free himself from the daily grind and dilemmas of field work. Moreover, he can specialize in his favorite area or, if he so desires, do intensive work, frequently with the aid of research grants, without being mired down in the "lower depths" of the field.

Beyond this he can, in hypothetical terms, define policy, "solve" world and national issues, and advise the lowly field worker without having to bear the responsibility for or do the pedestrian legwork necessary to implement his decisions. His is the best of all possible worlds within the field of social work.

9. Finally, the social worker can escape the pressures of first-line field work by specializing in administration or supervision. He becomes an expert on paper work, administrative rules and regulations, budget making, fund raising, and dealing with lay boards and governmental bodies. In doing so he shifts the locus of his interests from the world of the client to that of the world of the agency, or to the world of the funding agency or the lay board. He rationalizes this shift with the argument that solutions to the problems of the client (who increasingly becomes an abstraction) require more funds, more positions, and more expert planning, supervision,

and program development. And he is that expert in these areas.

The ideology of humanitarian service and of professionalism becomes the working tool of the upper administrative specialist. He uses his technical knowledge to make the laymen feel inadequate; his moral superiority to "blackmail" the funding agency and lay boards to increase budget and staffs; and his knowledge of the "higher realities" to coerce his professional staff to do work which is often regarded as unattractive, unprofessional, or immoral by that staff.

In part, these administrative practices are necessary if an agency is to operate; they are an accommodation necessary to implement the basic goals and plans of the profession. Field workers, however, tend on almost a standard basis to feel that their upper and middle administrative officials are careerist sell-outs. They feel that the bosses use the ideologies, the clients, and their staffs as stepping stones to better and bigger jobs, and as means of carving out or creating empires. In moments of irony they spend considerable time mimicking the double rhetoric of social work, from which no one is ever fired. Instead, one is given the opportunity to develop one's interests and career in areas more conducive to his interests, personality, or flair. Individuals "share" their interests instead of talking. Subordinates do not disagree; they resist or have problems, especially authority problems. Clients are never manipulated, they are involved. And authority does not exist. Obedience is defined as cooperation. Practice in linguistic virtuosity not only expresses irony, it is also training.

All these "patterns of adjustment" represent possible responses to the extreme confrontation between ideals and realities. When an individual makes one of these forms of adjustment, it becomes his occupational personality. To the extent that his underlying psychological factors predispose him to these patterns of adjustment, his occupational personality may become a stable one. In other cases, an individual can change his pattern of response by moving from one agency to another. Since these adjustments are responses to social and ideological developments in his field, it is difficult to blame an individual for his response or the field for its collective response. Moreover, within the field there are some, though their number may be small, who are selfless, dedicated, and skillful in getting through to their clients *despite* the obstacles. Others within administrative, specialized, or academic and research fields make vital and important contributions to their field despite these difficulties.

THE STRUCTURE OF WORK IN AN EMERGING POVERTY PROGRAM

OUR DISCUSSION of the occupational characteristics of the field of social work sets the stage for a discussion of community action programs designed to deal with problems of delinquency and poverty in the ghetto. The recent growth and expansion of these programs not only throw light on the dilemmas and contradictions between ideals and stubborn realities but also focus on the creation and routinization of new organizations in the area of social services.

While the author has been personally involved in a number of poverty programs, the following discussion focuses on problems which have been found endemic to a cross section of the country's 1,200 community action programs.

A vast number of present community action programs came into existence under the aegis of the President's Committee on Juvenile Delinquency and Youth Crime, headed by the then Attorney General Robert F. Kennedy. Under this program the President's Committee sought out local community leaders in urban ghettos, and encouraged them to organize themselves into permanent committees which would study the problems of their community and work out a detailed plan for combatting juvenile delinquency and youth crime. The President's Committee, together with private foundations and municipal governments, would then finance the research and planning phase (usually lasting from one to three years) of the projects. Once a program proposal was completed, arrangements to finance the operating phase would be envisaged. In this report we will be dealing only with the research and planning phases of such a program.

The local leaders who are involved in such programs include attorneys, ministers, social workers, government officials, politicians, teachers, and heads of city-wide agencies. In the ghetto community, unlike in society at large, the leaders of the community have relatively modest incomes. There are no multimillionaires whose interest in philanthropy represents a form of *noblesse oblige* and disinterested concern for the community. In the ghetto all leaders are engaged. Many of them are on the boards of these community action programs and see the program as an opportunity to get a well-paid job (under $20,000 per year) in this or other programs, to get patronage for their friends, to impress city hall by their loyalties, and to make political hay in their own community by fighting city hall and the "alien power structure" of the society at large. In addition the development of a new community action program in the ghetto disturbs the existing balance of leadership within a ghetto community which, although underorganized, has many claimants to leadership whose claims are based on the general lack of followers of all would-be leaders. The existing church, political, and social service leaders see in a new community action program a threat to their existing leadership. Some of these threatened leaders serve on the board of the infant organization and attempt to arrange for an infanticide. Others representing agencies which hope to control the moneys that they imagine to be forthcoming serve to direct the new organization so that it becomes a funding agency for their own organization. Others sit back and wait to feel how the wind blows. They will oppose or support the new organization depending on their estimate of whether there will be a live or a still birth and on the political strength of its actual parents or its godparents.

In all community action programs, the initial phases are carried out by a volunteer, unpaid lay board which represents all interested parties in the community but which has no paid permanent staff or executive arm of its own. An initial problem occurs when the supporters of the new community action program propose that it be incorporated and separated from its parent organization by giving it financial and legal independence and a staff that is responsible to the new organization and to no other group. The decision to incorporate and to create an independent staff is a crucial one. In all cases of such programs in the past five years where no independent staff has been created, the community action program was doomed to failure because no executive action could be taken. Instead, perpetual board meetings became the substance of the program. The decision to create a new corporation, however, results in a new organizational and power force in the community. In some cases the new organization can be created only if it "pays off" the old coordinating committee by promising it consulting or service contracts for little or no services.

When a new organization with a full-time staff is created, the qualifications and social base of the full-time paid executive director are crucial. Members of nonpaid boards immediately apply for the job, which, because of low salaries in the ghetto community, is one of the highest paid jobs in the community. If such a board member gets the job, he and his previous organization or sponsor become a dominant power in the community, and all other groups in the community may line up against him and the organization, and community-wide warfare ensues.

Usually the new executive director is selected because he has no political base in the community. He is generally an experienced government bureaucrat or social worker who sees in the new organization an opportunity either to create a new empire or to solve problems that no previous organization has solved. Typically, the outside executive director is not given sufficient powers of selecting and controlling his staff or of firing it. He is given, in addition, little budgetary independence. Thus the executive board controls all details of the executive operation of the organization. As a result, selecting a staff involves the total politics of the board and of the community. In addition, newly created social work, research, and administrative jobs are of great importance in a ghetto community, where jobs that pay professional-scale salaries are a rarity. Also, since educational opportunities are limited and there have been few professional jobs in the ghetto community, there is a dearth of qualified candidates. Thus, there are hundreds of applicants for the few well-paid professional jobs in the new organization, but very few applicants are qualified. The new organization, designed according to the statements of its board, to solve the fundamental problems of the community, attracts, in addition to professionals, ideologists who see in the new organization and the new positions opportunities to implement their ideologies. Thus the new organization, after months of screening, interviewing, and negotiating, will include among others professional careerists, members of the black bourgeois, Black Muslims, Maoists, Fidelistas, and other "new leftists," civil rightists of various organizational persuasions, and a few whites who are themselves members of minority groups and who may either represent their own minority group or be professional technicians without an apparent ideology except for their devotion to their field and the professional opportunities that derive from its practice. They are anomalies in a ghetto community where all other activities are charged with ideological significance.

As a result of these ideological commitments, each professional staff member comes to the new organization with a prepackaged program. The Black Muslim is oriented toward attacking any white power structure; the Maoist is oriented to educate and organize the youth and the community to create a revolution. The civil rights ideologist wants to organize demonstrations.

The executive director is committed to getting the new organization through its research and planning phases, and to getting "funded" on an operating basis by those organizations which have the funds. He faces two alternatives. He can look to existing sources of funds, governmental and foundational, and attempt to design programs that these agencies are prepared to finance. If he operates in this manner his program is likely to be remedial and conservative, since very few foundations or governments are likely to finance revolutions or violent demonstrations. He may, however, in attempting to please the hoped-for financial sponsors, become less daring and imaginative than the would-be sponsors desire. He may develop the Maginot Line psychology of copying past programs, when the sponsors are looking for new programs.

On the other hand, he may attempt to blackmail the white "power structure." He may directly or indirectly suggest that failure to get his funding will be evidence of discriminatory racism, the desire to perpetuate second-class citizenship for the ghetto citizen, and lack of good faith. In addition, he may invoke the memory of past race riots in the ghetto and the possibility of future ones. He may breathe a sigh of relief at the Watts riots, because these lend urgency to his demands for funds. He must be careful in the way he suggests the threat of a race riot. If he reports that conditions are so unsettled in the community that only a massive program under his direction can avoid a riot, he may succeed. If he suggests that *he* or some organization under his direction is going to promote a race riot, then he risks outliving his usefulness. The boundaries between psychological blackmail, which plays on the guilt and fear of the white liberal and politician, and direct threats and incitement to riot is a subtle and narrow one. Only the possession of the greatest skill in the arts of public relations prevents the most effective and subtle strategy from becoming a boomerang.

It is thus better that the action of the nationalistic and activist race leaders be independent of the community action leader. The activists shake the tree, and the community action people pick up the apples. Unfortunately at times, the activists would like to share in the apples. They enter the area of community action programs, bring threats of violence with them, and cause white politicians and liberals to fear that they are financing revolutions against themselves.

When the ideologist enters into paid work as a "professional" in a community action program, he is entering the world of bureaucracy. He is expected to do a narrow technical job with professional competence according to policy directives worked out by his superiors, the board, as interpreted and passed down by the executive director.

Unfortunately or fortunately, the ideologist sees himself as having a policy that derives from an ideological reference group, which is of absolute importance. The board and all other ideologists are wrong; and it is his absolute mission to develop, expand, indoctrinate, and apply his extraorganizational ideology within the framework of the new organization. Beyond this, he sees narrow professional work as petty detail, much beneath him, for which he has little talent or aptitude. The only techniques that he knows are techniques of agitating, exhorting, and propagandizing, against a real or imagined enemy. Beyond this, he is an organizer of demonstrations, sit-down strikes, and protest meetings.

When he enters the poverty program the ideologist finds that as a professional he does not make policy; it is handed down to him. He is expected to be a petty clerk. Moreover, the policies he is expected to carry out are policies of accommodation. The programs considered and devised by who he considers to be sell-outs, corrupt politicians, and black bourgeoisie, are programs that call for the poor to settle for tokens and handouts and enable them to be satisfied with a minimal bribe for silence. To the ideologist many of the leaders of the programs are thought to receive bigger rewards.

As a result the ideologists employ the only techniques they know against the poverty program in order to make it do a more effective job, as they define it.

Thus the internal atmosphere of the program, in many cases, is one of internal warfare. For months, the executive director will attempt to get the staff to do its professional job, that of drafting a fundable program. But the ideologists will spend months, from staff meeting to staff meeting, cutting down each proposal that does not go deep enough, is not radical enough, or is a form of tokenism. They will propose programs that are "revolutionary" in their impact and denounce the professionals as Uncle Toms when such programs are rejected. They will go out into the streets and attempt to organize community groups to bring pressure on the board of directors and the executive director to implement their revolutionary programs.

Of course, the ideologists come from a number of ideological camps, and a part of the internal warfare is directed at each other. At times this warfare results in near violent interchanges between staff members; and among a relatively small staff of five to seven members, at any one time there may be three to four cliques each of whose membership shifts on a day-to-day or week-to-week basis.

The executive director, however, prevents these cliques from becoming the basis of fraternal warfare. Since he is the major target for their animus, all cliques can unite in their opposition to the tokenism of the board as embodied by the executive director. The executive director is paralyzed by the ideological atmosphere of this staff. He sees week after week going by, in which the only results of the organization are ideological debates. He suspects, rightfully, that the ideologists on his staff are using ideological discussion and debate as a means of not doing the professional job for which they were employed and for which, he suspects, they are incompetent. In addition to spending vast amounts of time on ideological issues and personal organization of the community, the staff spends vast amounts of time writing memos. The substance of these memos is that they cannot do the job they are given because some other staff member or the executive director has not done something which is a prerequisite to the job. Since all the jobs are circular and involve everyone, no one can do his job.

The executive director is responsible for seeing that the total job is done, so his increasing sense of panic is totally understandable. In some cases he would like to fire his entire staff, but he cannot do so because, first, the board has never given him the right to hire and fire; second, to fire the staff would be to admit that his initial hiring recommendations were wrong, and third, he cannot admit to the board that his staff is rife with dissension and internal warfare and that nothing is being done. The board, however, will find it all out anyway. The executive director will attempt to escape the dilemma by hiring consultants on a daily basis at a high daily fee; their personal loyalty to him is assured by the fact that the fee is revocable. He will attempt to use the consultants to do the job that his staff is incapable of doing, and to use their skills at internal warfare against those of the staff. Such a procedure is extremely expensive and causes a drain on the budget. Moreover, the board of directors frowns upon the idea of having outside consultants, who have political bases outside the community, receive such rich financial plums.

Ultimately the staff will charge that the executive director is incompetent, making its representation to the board. The board may reject the charge but will be unwilling to fire the staff, which may cause a scandal. In addition there are many enemies of the organization (some of whom are on the board) waiting for scandal to erupt.

The problem is resolved when the executive director realizes that if the project continues at its present level, no final report or proposal will be written. He further realizes that, regardless of its cause, he will be held responsible for the failure. He thus resigns. The pattern of the "resignation" of the original executive director appears to be a necessity in poverty programs. It serves to educate the board to the idea that an executive director needs the authority to implement his and the board's decisions. Only when he has this authority can he be held responsible for the failure if and when it occurs. By this time, six months have passed out of the year of the project's contract. It takes a month to get a new executive director, during which time the staff members, free from the necessity of attacking the executive director, attack one another and the chairman of the executive board, who steps in to "keep the ship afloat" in the interim.

Candidates for the post of executive director tend to investigate the history of the organization while their own past work is being investigated by the board. Despite this there is a superabundance of candidates, few of whom are "qualified."

On the basis of their investigation, the candidates are inclined to ask for more authority, including the authority to hire and fire staff. The board is forced, on the basis of its past experience, to surrender to its new executive director the authority which it would not give to the original one. In this way, the board loses some of its authority in the community to a professional bureaucrat, who has a staff he now can control, and allows the new director to create its own political base in the community. The opportunity to create that base arrives in the response of the new executive director to the attempts of city hall to take over the community action program.

Initially, we have pointed out how the community action program came into existence under the sponsorship of the President's Committee on Juvenile Delinquency. It received an initial grant from that body to get organized. The assassination of President Kennedy resulted in a total change in the political and administrative climate of poverty in America. After President Johnson took control of the administration, there was for a year a period of marking time until the new leadership situation "worked itself out." Robert Kennedy resigned from all his federal offices, including the chairmanship of the President's Committee, and Sargent Shriver, his replacement, was slow to define a new policy.

The new regime radically redefined the context of community action and poverty programs. One could conclude that Robert Kennedy used his position as chairman of the President's Committee as a means of creating a new political machine based upon direct connection with, and financing by the President's Committee of, local community (grass-roots) elites, and on the bypassing of conventional political and governmental machinery. City and state governmental apparatus as well as the regular democratic party machinery were bypassed. The new alliance was to be a direct, personal one, in which new ethnic and political forces were to be brought into politics under the personal sponsorship of the Attorney General in programs paid for by the budget of the President's Committee. There is a distinct possibility that had it not been for the assassination, Robert Kennedy might have revolutionized politics in America.

As it was, the machine that Kennedy was in the process of creating fell apart, and when Attorney General Kennedy became Senator Kennedy he found himself an outsider, a would-be ethnic and urban working-class hero who was barred from the conventional machinery of rewarding his friends by hostile local, state, and national administrations that wanted to cut him down to size. From here on, Senator Kennedy would be forced to use the public relations of the outsider as a substitute for administrative and budgetary control as an insider that he had enjoyed in the Kennedy administration.

President Johnson, after he had time to take over the reins of government, instituted a policy that was just the opposite of the Kennedys' policy. First, because of a superior ability to get along with Congress, he received vastly greater budgets for the attack on poverty than did his predecessor. Second, he focused his attack on poverty in general and not on delinquency or area redevelopment as separate programs. Third, he relied on the use of the conventional party machinery as well as on local and state administrations, especially those controlled by the Democratic Party.

The new policy altered the context of community action programming exactly in relation to these three changes in political and administrative context. Program planners, hoping to get federal funds, could now shift their focus from juvenile delinquency and youth crime to the over-all problems of ghetto poverty. However, they were limited to the specific features of the Economic Opportunity Act and other similar legislation, rather than to the looser and more experimental (but smaller-budgeted) programs of the President's Committee.

More important, the greater budgets and the new opportunities for local participation made cooperation by local government all the more desirable. The new anti-poverty monies became to mayors, municipal politicians, and department heads a vast new source of patronage and a new source of funds to finance existing programs (with the federal budget instead of the local budget). It also meant that present municipal programs (like secondary education and welfare) could be expanded with federal funds. Finally, local political leaders could redeem promises to ethnic and economic minorities with federally financed programs.

As a result, in almost all metropolitan areas the mayors set up anti-poverty boards which were designed to devise, plan for, and administer programs that could be undertaken by the new bounty of federal Anti-Poverty Programs. These new local-government-sponsored anti-poverty programs came into conflict with the community action organizations created earlier at the invitation of the President's Committee. The community-based organizations were independent of city hall and had developed their own local political bosses, their own systems of patronage, and their own programs. City hall had continually waged war on such organizations as Haryou-Act and Mobilization for Youth as being communistic and mismanaged agitators and troublemakers. At the same time, city hall had to support these organizations financially if for no other reason than that their grass-roots involvement influenced or controlled many voters in their communities.

In the particular organization we are considering, the new interest in poverty planning by city hall came during the time the local community action corporation was presumably drawing up its own plans. The board and staff of the local community planning program were firmly convinced that the mayor's anti-poverty board was planning to delay and sabotage their efforts in order to prevent the program from coming into being as an operating organization. Evidence for such sabatoge was to be found in delays in authorizing the employment of necessary staff and the expenditure of funds previously allocated, and in interminable delays in the approval of programs and procedures developed by the community planning organization.

Evidence that these were acts of sabatoge was confirmed in a number of ways. First, it was discovered that all local community-based anti-poverty corporations were subject to the same delays, interference, and obstruction. From the standpoint of city officials, it might be argued that the delays were caused by the administrative and fiscal shortcomings of the local organization, and by the fact that the city anti-poverty board was madly trying, at the same time, to develop its own program. However, when the mayor's anti-poverty board announced its own program, it became clear that there was no place in the new scheme of things for the local independent community action organization. The original plans called for the creation, in each poverty area, of a city-appointed and city-staffed community action program. The independents were given a choice of being absorbed or being liquidated. All patronage and expenditure would thus go through city hall, and no local organization would have an independent political base.

This was the situation that confronted the new executive director of one of the local community action organizations. Not only was there internal chaos among his staff; not only was part of the board allied with city administration and rival organizations against the local organization; but the city administration was engaged in an all-out onslaught against the organization.

Realizing this, the executive director organized a committee to save the independent community action program. The committee was recruited from the local politicians (Democrats and Republicans), ministers, teachers, and other public-spirited community residents. The executive director, together with dependable members of the board, arranged to organize the committee, but the executive director was not a member of the committee. The staff was not involved in these arrangements because it was considered to be politically unreliable. Thus the committee was the result of a "spontaneous" movement of the community to save its local anti-poverty program.

There were organized and covered by the press "mass meetings" in which the mayor's anti-poverty board and the deputy mayor were denounced by speaker after speaker as racists, politicians, dictators or despoilers of the poor, who were trying to cheat the poor of their money by concentrating it at city hall. Each speaker attempted to outdo the others in his identity with his community and the poor. As far as can be gathered, all the speakers and almost all the members of the audience were of the middle and upper classes of the community. A congressman, up for election, spoke of his past contributions to the Negro and the poor and was denounced by "outside" civil rights group members in the audience for being white and for not having gone far enough. During the demonstration the audience responded more and more to the denunciation of city hall and the deputy mayor, so that the air of hostility evoked by the speakers was almost tangible. The meeting received a good press and was followed up by a series of interviews and releases in which the "community" presented its case against city hall through the newspapers. In addition, petitions were gathered throughout the community, and delegations visited city hall. Members of the community action staff and its board also served on a city-wide committee of representatives of local (President's Committee-created) community action organizations, which denounced the mayor's anti-poverty board. In doing so they received the oratorical help of Adam Clayton Powell, Senator Kennedy, and any number of other congressmen, who might have been interested in the welfare of their constituents as well as in preventing city hall from capturing all the political benefits of the federal budget.

The local community leaders, who were self-selected, claimed to be the only ones entitled to speak for the poor, and charged that elected political leaders were unable to speak for the poor. The poor, at the time, were not talking. The total volume of noise, statements, charges, by local leaders, national leaders, social workers, and self-selected leaders of the poor was so great that the mayor's anti-poverty board was forced to relent. "Representatives of the poor," that is, officials of independent anti-poverty programs were co-opted onto the executive board of the mayor's anti-poverty program. And as the election neared, city hall promised the community its own independent anti-poverty program through its own community action program.

The results of this demonstration of ability to organize the community to pressure for the local anti-poverty program were manifold.

First of all, it appeared that the future of the community-sponsored program was assured if it could devise a program that was respectable in form. Second, for the first time in history, the "community" had organized itself in a self-conscious and sustained manner or make its voice heard in the public opinion of the city. It helped, it is suspected, to defeat the deputy mayor in his attempt to gain the Democratic nomination for mayor and helped to defeat the Democratic candidate for mayor. The mayor's anti-poverty board was "too little and too late" in its accession to minority-group opinion.

It must be remembered that the political effectives were

only a segment of the elite of the community. Moreover, their political effectiveness was a product of the organizational effectiveness of a paid official, the executive director, who was not a resident of the community. Finally, the political development of the community resulted in an ideology that all those who opposed the community action program were, if white, racists, and if not white, saboteurs. The ideology of the entire civil rights movement was preempted into the drive for funding of one special organization.

Once the political predominance of the community action program was established, then it became clear that it would become the chief recipient of all anti-poverty funds coming into the community. All other groups in the community began to make presentations to it for anti-poverty funds. Such requests came from adult sponsors of drum and bugle corps, owners of charm and beauty schools, as well as heads of local organizations that had been up until this time trying to sabotage the community action organization.

The executive director, now with the appearance of total fiscal control over the community, began to set up criteria that would force all applicants for city, state, and federal anti-poverty funds to submit their requests to his organization. He and his board would approve or deny these requests. He did not succeed. The leaders of the larger organizations in the community who were submitting their own proposals for federal funds resisted these demands but went underground in opposing the community action program. Battles for independent programs were fought behind closed doors and were to reappear later, when the community action program became vulnerable for other reasons.

In the meantime, with a new optimism engendered by the organization's political victory, the executive director attempted to complete its programs. Instead, however, of completing its original contractual assignment for the plan of a long-term community action program, a new direction was undertaken. This was to develop a crash summer program aimed at avoiding an expected summer riot. The aims of this program were drawn up by the mayor's anti-poverty board. They included an attempt to get maximum involvement of a maximum number of youths and adults in programs that would keep them busy, regardless of what else the programs accomplished. Aiming for a summer program meant attempting to do in two months what the organization had been unable to do in ten months.

Under the spur of the new authority by the executive director to fire and hire, the enthusiasm engendered by an impossible deadline, and the forced cooperation of the mayor's anti-poverty board, the staff threw itself wholeheartedly into the development of the summer program.

The staff worked day and night with unequaled energy; but its exhilaration by the intense action was tempered by a sense of burlesque. Its members regarded the programs they drafted as silly, as irrelevant to anything but tapping funds from the city. Some were designed to augment the financial resources of other organizations. None were designed, in the opinion of the staff, to solve any of the basic problems of the community.

The final report for the summer program thus contained a vast mixture of unrelated programs, extremely unstructured in conception, which would require vast staffs of trained professionals, who were not available, and months to organize, which also were not available.

Several of the permanent staff were fired for obvious incompetence in the period during which the report was prepared. Several resigned over basic differences of philosophy. One resigned over "personality" differences with the executive director. One staff member was "fired or resigned" because he could not help but continue to organize the youth for a radical upheaval of the community. By the time the first year was over, the entire original staff had either resigned or been fired. By the end of the second year, those who had "fired" the original staff were themselves fired, a phenomenon characteristic of most poverty programs.

They were replaced by a new staff which was entirely different in character and background. None of the new staff were ideologists. Some were well trained, as well as personal friends of the executive director. A few former board members later were promoted to full-time paying jobs on the staff of the organization.

The new staff had an entirely different orientation to the program than did the old one. They did not eschew administration; rather, they loved it. They created forms in triplicate, procedures, titles, administrative directives, and policy directives galore. They were concerned with carpeting, air conditioning, and the prerogatives and accouterments of the office. They enjoyed staff meetings and conferences and wrote memoranda and minutes. They were anxious about "covering" themselves and uncovering the mistakes of others. To these clean-cut resemblers of Madison Avenue, "administration" was a way of life, equal in importance to public relations and the creation of "images." The major criterion after the development of new programs was their ability to attract favorable and immediate response in the community and in the wider urban society. Such programs involved maximal use of parades, singing, dramatic performances, and artwork. The guided tour for visiting dignitaries was the major result of the program. But another major result was the avoidance of a summer riot. If this was the purpose of the program, the program was a success.

During this period, in response to a ruling by Sargent Shriver, plans were made to recruit members of the actual poor onto the board. The ruling that actual poor people (earning $3,130 a year or less) were to make up a third of the members of the board astounded the old board members and the executive director, who had previously regarded themselves as the representatives of the poor. But they complied gracefully, recruiting members of the poor but replacing certain of these new members who were militant. However, they did not hold elections, which in principle would have given the poor actual power and independence.

A few of the critics of the program who were hired as consultants were thus silenced.

It is not my intention to describe in detail the actual operation of the summer program, because much of my knowledge is secondhand. I will attempt only such description as is necessary to complete the picture.

The summer program did get under way on schedule. Because of delays in evaluating and approving the summer proposal at city hall, the starting date of the actual operation of the program was only ten days after the program was approved by the mayor's anti-poverty board. During those ten days the community action organization attempted to create an operating organization. It recruited a staff of teachers, social workers, administrators, researchers, music counselors, psychologists, youth and community organizers, and dozens of other workers. Thousands of would-be program participants were interviewed and screened. These included unwed mothers, school dropouts, truants, and youth and adult applicants for job training, for "leadership" training, and for recreational programs. At the same time curricula and program content were supposed to be developed, and an administrative and financial structure was to be created.

It is not surprising that much was left undone. Ten days is a short time in which to set up a dozen or more programs administrating the diverse activities of over five thousand program participants.

In some cases, programs were set up and no participants were available. Thus the truants' program was put into operation, but there was no time available to recruit truants. This had been overlooked in the haste. After the program staff had stood around for a week, a storefront minister recruited several hundred children for the program; no one inquired whether they were truants or not. An investigation failed to reveal a curriculum or any attempt to assign students to teachers. Students dropping into the first empty room in sight had a different teacher each day. In many cases the teachers did not know who their students were since there had been no systematic assignment of students and teachers to classes. No testing was undertaken to place students according to ability, and teaching level was not related to the level of ability of students. The teachers were instructed to develop curricula in nonteaching hours. Some (about half) resented these demands because they viewed their job as a summer vacation and refused to cooperate with the eager beavers who did work on curricula. Some of the Negro teachers would not cooperate with white teachers and vice versa. Both groups fought their administrators. Researchers were involved in battles with both groups, with project administration, and with their own supervisors.

In the meantime, the students, in response to the confusion, began to drop out of the program. By midpoint in the program students were hard to find. Since there was no one to teach, teachers began to disappear, spending vast parts of the day in coffee shops and parks. It strained the ingenuity of project administrators to assemble and continue classes that would appear to be operative whenever a visiting delegation was taken through on a guided tour.

An adult job-training program was set up that evoked a high degree of initial enthusiasm on the part of adults participating. One program was in upholstery crafts; it was set up because a seasonally unemployed upholsterer had applied for a job training upholsterers. The program was created on the basis of the availability of the teacher, despite the fact that upholstery is a declining industry, requires several years of apprenticeship, and operates under a closed shop of "lily-white" unionism. The trainees, under the illusion that training would produce jobs, embarked upon it with enthusiasm. About seventy-five trainees were involved under the direction of one teacher.

Similarly, an automobile mechanics course was set up. Between twenty-five and forty trainees were enrolled at any one time under the supervision of one instructor. Tools and automobiles were provided by the students, since it was difficult to purchase these through channels. A strike against this project was considered by the trainees, because to the best of their knowledge there was no placement service attached to it. Some trainees felt that they were being used in a fake program to keep the administrators happy. Their pay while training ($1.35 per hour) was not sufficiently attractive (it paid less than welfare) to encourage support for a program that would leave them "holding the bag," without jobs, after the program was over. The strike was narrowly averted, owing in part to the intervention of a researcher, who was later fired for lack of loyalty to the project.

The only persons who knew the full range of operation of the entire program were the various members of the research department. Most of these were graduate students in the social sciences, though a few were untrained "political" appointments. The majority had been previously involved in CORE, SNCC, or SCLC, and had been active in civil rights demonstrations in the South. Several had spent time in southern jails. As they observed their respective projects, they became increasingly disenchanted. Some began to feel that the entire program was fraudulent but hoped that research might improve it. Some members of the research staff felt that the executive director and research director were increasingly anxious less the research reports of the program's operations would be its most severe indictment. The research director ordered all research projects stopped and substituted for these a number of research instruments which one might describe as having "face fraudulence"; that is, even an untrained reader could see that use of the research instruments could produce only favorable results. In addition, the researchers were given a half-dozen forms to fill out which were purely administrative in purpose (they were expected to account in writing for each hour worked). This increased their disenchantment.

Rumors that the researchers were planning to demonstrate or strike against the project began to circulate. An outside investigator was called in to examine the situation. He recommended that all unnecessary paper work be stopped, that the researchers concentrate on only those jobs which could reasonably be completed. The replacement of the research director was recommended by the investigator. This was not found feasible. In the meantime the outside investigator attempted to convince the young rebels that professionals do not strike or demonstrate against their own organization. If they cannot secure redress for their complaints within their own organization, they should resign. The strike or demonstration was thus squashed.

The executive director took the opportunity of the investigation to force the resignation of the assistant research director, who, he believed, contrary to the report of the investigator, was responsible for agitating the researchers to protest. He also decided not to reappoint any of the entire research staff at the termination of their initial contract: in effect he would fire all of them. This applied to the researchers who had opposed strikes or demonstrations as well as those who had not. On the last day of their employment, the executive director invited a group of five researchers, including some of the leaders of the aborted strike, to "thank" them for their work and to ask for their suggestions. The researchers volunteered by suggesting that the entire project was ineffective, mismanaged, and staffed by "traitors" to the poor.

One researcher, in order not to embarrass the others, staged a personal sit-down strike in the executive director's offices, after his colleagues had left. The sit-down strike took place in the midst of a meeting between the executive director and a delegation from the Urban League. Staff officials pleaded for the recalcitrant sit-downer to leave voluntarily and then called the police. When other researchers heard that their colleague had staged a sit-down, they went back to the executive director's office and began to bang on the door in order to join their friend in his sit-down strike. They were locked out. The embittered former assistant research director, hearing of the strike, began calling newspapers with the story. The papers did not print the story.

The sit-down striker, who had been previously jailed as a civil rights demonstrator in Mississippi, decided to terminate his strike after two hours; as he left, he passed in the hall the police officer summoned to arrest him. Since he had left, no arrest was made. Peace was restored, and the project went into a dormant stage for six months until the funds came through to finance its regular program.

PART III

*

Ethics in Nonprofit Organizations

ACADEMIA

OUR DISCUSSION of the structure of several nonprofit organizations together with the discussion of the organization of work and the higher ideologies of these organizations provides a framework for the analysis of ethics in these organizations.

We have indicated that academia justifies itself by a superior morality based on the Disinterested Search for Truth, which places itself above the muck and mire of ordinary existence, especially that of the businessman. We have also indicated that work is organized in the university to allow individuals to justify their moral claims. That is, they are allowed to search for truth, because there is a large amount of time available for that task. When they fail, they emphasize teaching, contract research, and administrative service as means of justifying their existence.

In a sense, any failure to use the time made available for writing or research is a violation of the ethical norms implicit in the ideology of the academician. He has reneged on the promise of his ideology. Academicians, however, do not perceive lack of productiveness as an ethical failure. Productivity among the productive is conceived as a basis for prestige and a validation (in almost Freudian terms) of one's manhood. Lack of productivity is also viewed as a psychological problem of the unproductive and a basis for condescension, pity, or derision. Excess productivity is viewed by the unproductive as a product of a neurosis (promiscuity) or as an aggressive desire to humiliate one's colleagues. It is unethical, since it violates the norms of restriction of output in the academic shop.

The productive do not accept the ideologies of teaching or

administrative services as justification for nonproduction. They feel they are an alibi. They feel that these "subsidiary" functions can be achieved without sacrificing productivity. For the others, the ideology of teaching and administrative service allows them to justify themselves despite the failure to fulfill what all regard as the primary purpose of their occupational existence. The academic community splits and divides itself on these, and other, issues.

Yet the ethical issues involved in productivity are subtle ones, below the surface of most discussion and conflicts. Other ethical problems are more manifest.

ETHICS INVOLVING EXPLOITATION
OF STUDENTS

PERHAPS THE simplest and most obvious problems of ethics are those involving the exploitation of the student. To the public, the teacher exists to impart skills and knowledge to his students. It is not at all strange, however, that any professional should feel that the external world exists so that he can practice his professional skills upon it.

The student exists as a necessary source of income (teaching) and as a resource for free labor for the teacher. This is especially true for graduate students, since undergraduates are usually presumed to require too much training before they can be successfully exploited. A successful exploiter can become an amazingly recondite scholar familiar (in his books) with vast bodies of exotic materials simply by assigning a large number of graduate students to do his work for him. With good graduate students and administrative ability the great scholar can achieve world renown by intelligently posing a problem for his students and by being a good editor. This has been the basis of a vast number of scholarly books. And yet, one could argue that it is not exploitation. For the graduate student is, by such labors, given the opportunity to do independent, professional work under the guidance of a skilled professional. He learns, perhaps by the only way possible, what a researcher actually does. He may gain as much from the experience as does the exploiter.

What constitutes exploitation in such situations is the frequent unwillingness of the professor to get involved in the actual problems and the hard details of research work. There is a wide range of practice in this regard. The moral leper is the professor who assumes responsibility for the research by saying: "After all, I bear the full responsibility for the work by having my name on it." Some will resent and punish their students after the work is completed because they remind him of his indebtedness. And some students will go out of their way to make such reminders. The professor is normally expected to help the exploited graduate student get his Ph.D. and find him a job when he enters the job market. One of the severest forms of moral leprosy is for the professor to sabotage the student in his oral or written Ph.D. examinations (or to fail to support him) after he has exploited the student for several years. The ethical norm is, If a student is good enough to do the professor's work, he should be good enough to do his own. He is thus entitled to the Ph.D. Sabotaging the exploited student in his quest for a Ph.D. is thus reneging on an implicit bargain.

Moral leprosy may also take the form of keeping the student in a state of dependence. Ordinarily a student will grow in knowledge and competence, until he becomes the equal of his mentors. As he approaches equality, the more menial digging and clerical work involved in research is viewed by the student as increasingly unrewarding and onerous. At the same time, the growth of the student represents a loss of clerical assistance to the professor. The moral leper will stretch out for years the low-grade clerical work required of the student. In effect, the professor denies the growth and creates dependency, which is perhaps the most serious crime of all. The graduate student quite frequently is forced to rebel against the professor in order to achieve full academic manhood. His independence is celebrated all too frequently by bitterness, conflict, and resentment. In this sense the Freudian family drama, wherein the sons rebel against the father, is reenacted. It is not, however, a biological necessity. It occurs only when a strong "son" deals with a "father" who is too weak to permit his son's growth. Sometimes the phrase used to describe this process suggests femininity. Thus achieving intellectual independence is described as "cutting the umbilical cord."

Other forms of exploitation also exist. The professor may use undergraduates for low-grade clerical work from which it is not possible for the student to profit. He pays the student in grades or in attention for work a businessman might pay for in money. This is so common a practice that it is not regarded as a deviation from ethical norms except when the amount of work demanded makes it impossible for the student to meet other necessary commitments. Another form of exploitation of students is much more subtle. Many professors regard themselves as prophets or culture heroes. Some are only vain. By surrounding themselves with a group of inexperienced, admiring students, they create a cult or a claque. The professor has his captive audience.

This is attractive to both the professor and the student. The professor finds a group that takes him seriously, feeds his vanity, and thus he escapes from the isolation that exists because professors often cannot talk to one another. The student gets the opportunity to see and work closely with a culture hero. This is especially true if his own background is one of cultural poverty. In becoming a member of the cult or claque, he begins to live in the world of ideas, letters, and science. He acquires a new father and a new identity. He enters a wider world. If this is accomplished, it is perhaps a necessary stage in the growth of the neophyte academician. It becomes exploitation only when the culture hero attempts to restrict the growth of the neophyte to those ideas that he personally affirms. The student may be forced to rebel in order to escape from cultism as intellectual tyranny.

SEXUAL EXPLOITATION

THE DISCUSSION of material and psychological exploitation permits us to discuss the sexual morality of academia. Despite the layman's image of the college professor as sexless, an image perhaps based on religious origins of American colleges and the popular tradition reinforced by the mass media that books and beds are incompatible, professors are not much different from members of other occupations. A goodly number marry and have children. Every college has its share of extramarital peccadilloes. In fact, on the isolated college campus the discovery that a professor is having an affair with a colleague's wife constitutes an administrative problem. To relieve the tension caused by such a scandal, one party, usually the offending male, must resign. The fact that the "offender" is a valuable member of the staff is of secondary importance. In a number of cases, productive university departments have been broken up over just such scandals. Of course, many of the marriages were also broken up.

Almost as common is the faculty whore. Here we are speaking of the female student who married the professor twenty or more years of age older than she. The professor, either because of age or for other reasons, begins to lose his sexual potency, interest, or attractiveness precisely at the time when the wife ripens sexually. It is not infrequent that the wife will then have a series of affairs, or will be sexually promiscuous with a number of men, including faculty members. The faculty whore will be a cherished institution on the campus, with the entire faculty conspiring to prevent scandals, to delude the husband, and to delude the wives of involved husbands, while chuckling over the latest gossip concerning the whore's activities.

Again this is not peculiar to universities, except that in an isolated university town extramarital sexuality is often endogamous and thus threatening to the structure of the community.

What is more peculiar to the academic community is the sexual exploitation of neophytes. Since much of graduate and undergraduate training is of a handicraft nature, it involves close work between students and teachers. The teacher has much power over the future career and fate of the student, and the student is relatively powerless. Moreover, the older professor has the glamour of knowing the wider world, may be (at least in the eyes of the student) a celebrity, and is thus sexually attractive. In this respect the academic community is not unlike the theater or the movies, or even advertising, where the older elite can determine the life chances of neophytes, whether of the same or opposite sex.

To the professor in his thirties or older there is a great temptation arising out of working with young, enthusiastic, and apparently innocent youngsters who admire or worship him for his academic accomplishments. It is greater as the professor and his wife age. The wife may be physically less attractive than in her youth, and as the husband begins to develop the normal anxieties surrounding his own loss of potency, sexual exploitation of the student becomes a "natural" possibility, especially as graduate students often do not conceive of affairs with their professors as exploitation. In some schools the phrase "getting one's degree on her back" is a standard phrase, attesting to the informal social recognition of this form of ascent.

In other schools, professors compete in the seduction of graduate students, a competition which appears not to diminish their academic productivity. It represents a real tragedy when, because of differences in age, charm, or stature, one of the competitors is unable to maintain the pace.

In the first half of the century American colleges were racked with a series of scandals in which outstanding professors had to resign because they used the college equipment such as tabletops, labs, and pianos for purposes other than that for which they were intended. In other cases the scandals were avoided by informal administrative action (including marriage).

A typical case would involve the professor who is having an affair with the wife of his graduate assistant. Tiring of the wife, the professor arranges for the husband to receive a fellowship abroad in order that the wife will depart with her husband. Hearing that she is to be abandoned by her lover, the wife denounces him to her lover's boss, the department chairman. The department chairman is a man of low prestige and productivity while the lover is a professor of international fame in his field.

The department chairman is forced to take action, since

the alleged behavior, if proved, would constitute moral turpitude, a ground for dismissal, or, if made public, a scandal. The department chairman, with the wisdom of a Solomon, resolves the legal and ethical problems of the case by depriving the offending professor of the opportunity to teach his favorite course—advanced ethics.

With the rising moral tolerance of the second half of the twentieth century such moral dilemmas are less a problem. While the amount of sexual activity may well have increased, the tolerance of it has increased even more.* Thus the predominant solution is to look the other way. The ethical problem rather than the moral problem is involved in the uses of sexual immorality. For the professor to demand sexual submission as the price of a grade or degree would be unethical. For a student to barter his or her favors for a degree would also be unethical. In most cases, however, sexual bargains are not stated in such hard or bald terms that ethics becomes an issue.

For a professor to discard a student lover without granting her (or him) the degree would, however, be considered moral leprosy. The student, however, would have to do enough work for her (or his) degree to maintain appearances.

PLAGIARISM, THE THEFT OF IDEAS, AND THE ASSIGNMENT OF "CREDITS"

PRODUCTIVITY AND CREATIVITY represent the fulfillment of the claims of the ideology of the academic man. Therefore recognition as being productive or creative is central to the sys-

* Parents of undergraduates need not worry, because on a per thousand basis the number of such affairs is undoubtedly low. In part this is due to a high student-faculty ratio, in part to the timidity of students and the competition by other students of the opposite sex. In addition, the vast majority of professors, at any given time, are preoccupied with other matters.

tems of self-validation and to the rewards deriving therefrom. On this basis, plagiarism might be expected to be one of the most serious violations of an ethical norm in academia.

The difficulty is that it is hard to define plagiarism. In a legal sense, plagiarism means a word-for-word copying of another man's work. This is relatively rare. There have been a few cases (resulting in famous law suits) in which the plagiarist was clumsy enough not to change the language of the plagiarized work. Where this occurs the convicted offender is regarded as a pariah and finds it difficult to find a permanent academic position, despite the quantity and quality of his other work.

In other cases, a major professor is reported to have delayed publication of his students' work until he has completed his own book on the subject. This type of behavior, while only partially related to plagiarism, becomes the subject for gossip throughout this field (but has no other results). Publication of the results of students' research (usually in the professor's own language) is a standard procedure. The operative ethical norm is at least to acknowledge the help of the students and to cite their work if it is a dissertation or publication. Professors who fail to do so may be resented, gossiped about, and avoided. It is considered to be ethical to offer a junior authorship to students whose work the professor publishes. An ethical paragon would give his students editorial and consulting advice without extracting a coauthorship.

Simple cases of plagiarism are rare among professionals (though common among undergraduates). "Disguised plagiarism" or the "theft" of ideas is allegedly more common. The major form of such disguised plagiarism is paraphrasing a work available only in a foreign language. A major work in a foreign language that is "great" and relatively unknown can be the source of many original books and articles for professors whose major claim to scholarship is good taste and a knowledge of the foreign language in question. Again the boundaries of plagiarism are not clear. If the paraphraser cites the original but does not disclose the extent of his "borrowing" he may convey a false impression. Or he may cite the original along with forty other citations so that his apparent obligation to the one chief source is diluted. In this sense the old canard is true that "if you borrow from one source it's plagiarism, if you borrow from many it's research." At any event, conveying a false impression, either by omission or overcommission is a form of moral leprosy. It is known only to the cognoscenti who are familiar with the source. The translation of the original manuscript may of course reveal the extent of the borrowing, and in some cases it has been charged that translations were done as an act of aggression against the borrower. The charges may have been true.

Still more vague are the conscious and unconscious borrowings from one's peers. If one were to listen to the complaints of a vast number of relatively unproductive academicians the amount of theft of ideas is unlimited. Credit for the same work may be claimed by a half-dozen injured parties. Whether these are expressions of sour grapes or represent a reality is a matter of conjecture. One method of validating such claims for lost authorship is as follows. Creativity is likely to be an attribute of a man as much as of a work. Thus if the injured party claims creativity for someone else's publication and has done no creative work himself, there is reason to suspect the claim. If the alleged thief of ideas is creative in many areas, at least, he has good taste; and, at most, he is not a thief. In addition, a dullard may steal a good idea, but its development will reflect his personality as well as the originality of the idea.

Finally, one must conclude, if all the ideas reported stolen were actually stolen the world would be infinitely richer. For, as we have previously indicated, only good ideas are reportedly stolen; and there are too few good ideas in any field to support all the claims for theft. Despite this, a vast number of scholars go through their professional lives with a button on their lips, fearful that they might let slip a remark or an idea that might be useful to someone else. As long as the ideas are unexpressed, they are potentially useful.

The fear of revealing one's ideas prior to publication suggests a dilemma. A person who hears of or reads an idea that is useful to him is under the obligation to use it if by his using it his work or his field would benefit. In a sense he is obligated to "steal" the idea. The old motto that "ideas are not toothbrushes" still applies. His ethical obligation, however, is to give full and unstinting credit to those who wittingly or unwittingly are the source of useful ideas. This is difficult. In the first place a faulty memory (consciously or unconsciously) may obscure the source of the idea. Years may elapse between exposure and application. In this case, it is easy to attribute to oneself the origin of one's ideas. Nevertheless, authors who do not cite (where they can) the source of their ideas are considered unethical. Thus, after close to a hundred years it is fairly well established that Charles Darwin had read Alfred Russel Wallace's works on evolution and failed to cite them. Freud was aware that ideas similar to his own were present in the works of Nietzsche, Schopenhauer, Stirner, Schnitzler, and De Sade, some of which he may have read earlier. He deliberately did not reinvestigate those authors, in order to work out solutions to his own problems in terms of the materials available to himself. The originality of his own work is the best defense of his integrity. For even if he had "borrowed" these ideas, he went far beyond them. He made the ideas work and in doing so remade them into something new. And this is what creativity consists of.

Another form of "borrowing" of ideas results from the teacher-student relationship. The great teacher can be a source of a plentitude of ideas which he releases to his students naturally. He cannot help doing so. And the sensitive student cannot help but absorb the ideas. They become incorporated into his professional and intellectual armory and become the basis of his professional life. Of course, this is what teaching at its best is like and should be.

Many teachers are primarily verbal. They cannot or do not write the best of their work, but they do offer their ideas freely to their students. The student accepts them perhaps without realizing the extent of his indebtedness, until he comes to the point of being a professional. At that time, his self-esteem may prevent him from recognizing that many or most of his ideas are borrowed. If he begins to write and publish, especially if he writes well, he may achieve an outstanding reputation based upon the professor's ideas. The professor would not be human if he did not resent the recognition his student got for these ideas. He is likely to become estranged from his students precisely as they get recognition. In some cases he will attempt to deny them the recognition or impede the publication of their works. If he does, he becomes a moral leper in that he denies them growth. To defend himself the student may have symbolically "to cut the cord" or to "kill the totemic father." In doing so he may deny all obligation to his mentor and himself become a moral leper. The ethical student will give full public recognition to his mentor. Yet this is not a great gesture of self-renunciation. For he will still be categorized, if his work deserves it, as a productive or creative professional on the basis of the work done, no matter how much he bestows credit on others. If the professor depends on the recognition he achieves through his students, he gains the reputation of being a great teacher but not of being a great scholar. Being renowned as a great teacher will be of little solace if the student gains the reputation of being a great scholar. And yet, in the final analysis, it is for his own disability that the "great teacher" suffers. If he is capable of great ideas, it is his obligation to himself to write them up. If he does not, the failure (and it is only a personal one if his ideas do get disseminated through others) is his own.

The student cannot be blamed for absorbing good ideas. He can be blamed for not acknowledging their sources. In addition, his creativity is suspect if he depends on the ideas of only one man or if he does nothing but explicate the ideas of another. The development of knowledge depends on the borrowing of ideas, but in this process it is assumed that the borrower will modify, change, expand, alter, and combine, received ideas so that his work represents a cumulative development rather than mere replication. If nothing is added except "style" or illustration, then the student may get the reputation of being a moral leper or merely of being uncreative. At times he will be thought of as a popularizer or as a mere "journalist."

In all the above cases the distinction between creativity and productivity is a major factor. The ideology of scholarly pursuits exalts creativity, the creation of new ideas and concepts and the extension of combinations of older ideas to new areas. But we are increasingly aware that creativity is a psychological trait, a characteristic of the man as well as of his work. If this is true, then the failure to be creative is not a moral or ethical lapse but an unavoidable lack. Productivity is, however, a controllable phenomenon. Productivity involves doing valuable and useful work even though it results in no great innovation in concepts and ideas. The failure to be productive represents a moral or ethical lapse (as well as a psychological or administrative one) since productivity involves discretionary action over which it can be assumed the individual has some control. Thus the unproductive scholar must experience guilt or negative esteem. Productivity is a necessary substitute for creativity, though the notion that one is "merely productive" is difficult to face. The quest for "creativity" is thus an escape from the idea of "mere" productivity. It forces the worshiper of creativity to adopt "gimmicks," creative attitudes, and poses. It may sensitize him to ideas that are novel or that have possibilities of dramatic exploitation. He may become a brain picker. Again, the reputation of being a brain picker is likely to be harmful in some circles but does not overweigh a reputation based on the quality of the brains "picked" as represented by work actually done. Some brain pickers have little taste or sense in their brain picking or do little with the brains picked. Others will do substantial work. In short, despite the brain picking, they are productive.

A final difficulty in the ethics of creativity is represented by the social nature of creativity. It is rare that an individual will make a discovery "out of the blue." Work in almost all areas proceeds upon the basis of there being hundreds of men individually and collectively attacking common problems. They all borrow from their predecessors and from one another; they successively, by their failures, eliminate fruitless lines of research and develop other lines of inquiry and procedures for following through along these lines. The great innovation, the breakthrough, then usually represents the combination of a number of known elements or the application of newly emergent concepts to a problem that has been previously unresolved, or even more importantly to a problem whose definition is the discovery; that is, the discovery of a problem may be as important as the solution.

In each case, the act of creativity represents a *new* combination of old elements, the development of a *new* technique to solve an old problem, or the development of a *new* way of stating a problem in order to make it solvable.

In each approach, the creation is usually based upon the works of others. It is extremely rare that creation is a purely individual affair, although the creative person may have unique talents in perceiving the application or combination of familiar elements that results in a creation. As a result the creator and his professional peers are more aware of their dependence on others than are distant laymen. The "creator" is likely to be celebrated because his final step results in a dramatic perceivable breakthrough. Laymen need to symbolize creativity and the creator by imagining one dramatic act or one creative hero. In seeking these forms of simplification they are likely to neglect the hundreds of workers who made the creation possible. In celebrating the work of the creator they raise him to the level of a culture hero and bestow praise, prestige, publicity, and material rewards upon him. The hero achieves in overabundance some of the values to which his total career has been pointed. It would not be difficult for him to accept the layman's definition of creativity, to see it as the unique act of the supergenius. It would be easy for him thus to forget his intellectual obligations to all the others "upon whose shoulders he stood," or to be perfunctory or conventional in his acts or recognition of these others. It would be more difficult to go back to the lab, to do the same dull, plodding work which made his creation possible. The accepting of the role of a celebrity, symbol, or image by a young man and substituting it for the role of a substantive worker are viewed as a form of treason.

The social nature of creative process places ethical burdens on creative scholars, since only some steps in the total process of creation are rewarded. What is more, there is little agreement among professionals on the importance of the respective steps. In addition the social nature of the quest for knowledge means that a vast number of individuals will be working on a common problem, using as their common background the work of common predecessors. Thus it may be hard to differentiate at a given time between the work and the contributions of large numbers of workers. Their work necessarily resembles one another's. What appears to be plagiarism may be separate resolutions of the same problem. The result is confusion because some groups will hold back the release of findings until they are sure of the findings. Others who make a discovery later will announce it immediately because of pressures to achieve recognition either for themselves or for institutions whose publicity purposes they are forced to serve. As a result there are continual conflicts over the dates of discovery and dates of publication. The ethical imperative is to cite earlier work if known and to report accurately the date of discovery, an imperative as honored in its breach as in its observance.

Such conflicts, however, are relatively rare, but they are dramatic. Their rarity and drama are a product of outstanding but almost identical contributions that are made or announced within the same time period.

Similar though not so dramatic conflicts occur over less clearly defined issues. These conflicts usually do not result in public scandals, but they do result in a carefully nursed sense of injury which allows their holders to claim credit, in small circles, for work that others receive credit for in larger circles. These conflicts, however, allow the injured party to validate himself in terms of the ideology of productivity or creativity. He may even become a local hero in his university as the man who anticipated Keynes or Salk or Einstein, and so on. By such means, local reputations are made and sustained.

THE ETHICS OF INTERPERSONAL RELATIONSHIPS

IN ALL THE ABOVE, we have, to some degree, suggested norms governing interpersonal relationships. There are others that *specifically* govern interpersonal relationships. These are relatively few in number and cover a wide range of specific areas.

The simplest ones regulate discussion with students by faculty of other faculty members and of faculty affairs. The norm specifies that no faculty member should denigrate any other faculty member in public or before students. At the same time, faculty members are not supposed to air their differences with other faculty members over department policy or over different conceptions of their field or its findings. This latter point involves some problems, since intellectual differences are central to the fields in which academicians work. In any field, at the point where original work is being done, there are different approaches and different schools of thought which are antithetical and over which sharp conflicts arise and battle lines are drawn. Members of conflicting factions on the same faculty are supposed to make no personal references to their differences, though expressing their positions in impersonal terms with no reference to the opposing point of view is permissible among academicians of equal rank.

Needless to say, few academicians are able to maintain such high standards. Moreover, when a professor has established a personal cult among his students, he is closer to them than he is to the faculty. He uses his students to air his grievances against the faculty and is likely to "spill" departmental gossip and derogatory anecdotes to students. This is likely to make the student feel that he is "in" and is being treated as a mature professional. It contributes to his professional socialization. If, however, the student gossips to other students who belong to another professor's cult, the first professor risks being viewed as a moral leper.

It is, of course, permissible to gossip about professors at other schools provided that the gossip doesn't get back and that it is not too derogatory. A surprising amount of such interscholastic gossip does feed back and becomes the source of a sense of injury.

It is not "wise," of course, for a junior faculty member to air his differences with a senior faculty member or department chairman over issues which in other situations are legitimate subjects for discussion. Quite frequently, a strong department chairman will create a department whose membership will all be drawn from one "school" in his discipline. The department will have an official "line" and will consider all other "lines" as treason. The junior faculty member will be forced to curb his interests and suppress his training if they do not fall into the permitted area of academic freedom. Officially, penalizing a junior for his beliefs or academic approach is unethical. Unofficially, it is usual.

When a department does not specialize along "party lines," there will be conflicts built into its very table of organization. Each new staff member will be hired (usually after some conflicts) because of his academic approach. Penalizing a junior faculty member for holding to the approach for which he was hired is a double "crime." This, of course, happens not infrequently, owing to changes in the balance of power among senior professors (caused by death, resignation, promotions or changes in alignments or in support by the administration). Not to reappoint or promote a junior faculty member simply because he holds to his approach is considered scandalous. But the offending parties can and do defend themselves in terms of a higher morality, based upon the alleged incorrectness of the junior's approach or upon some other "objective" failure. Such scandals are a frequent and recurrent aspect of the academic community.

Equally, if not more, serious is the crime of recruiting students. The size of undergraduate classes is a measure to the administration of the value of a teacher to the school. The number of graduate students working on a thesis or dissertation is a measure of prestige among peers and also of value to the school.

A teacher who has difficulty in attracting students to his classes may lose face, a promotion if he has tenure, or a job if he does not. He may seek to solve this problem by attempting to teach required courses or to get his favorite course required. If he fails he may be forced to take unethical action. The forms of unethical action include reducing the work required of students, active recruiting, giving high grades, promising jobs or fellowships to students, and, in a few cases, paying them to take courses. All of these are forms of social leprosy, although paying students is undoubtedly the worst.

Securing fellowships, research assistantships, or scholarships for graduate students is not considered a form of moral leprosy since these are frequently related to the professor's research enterprises. In getting research funds for his own work, he provides the funds for research assistants who will naturally do their dissertation under his sponsorship. This of course produces resentment among professors who have or require no research funds to do their work. The use of such funds thus works in the same direction as bribery, recruiting, or promises of jobs or easy grades, but since the source of funds is legitimate, the activity is.

Most other forms of personal ethics concern department feuds. We have indicated two sources of such feuds. One involves differences over academic issues and schools of thought within the discipline. The other surrounds the necessity of being busy. The latter is more serious and usually includes the former. These feuds become the major basis for the way of life of significant numbers of the academic community.

The professor, perhaps in his youth, usually after he has received tenure, is able to repay some of his accumulated resentments by blocking the aspirations of his previous tormentor. He begins or joins a vendetta and can find a source of meaning in a life that either does not require him to work on his self-selected problems or serves as an alternative to such work. He has friends, allies, and enemies. Time can be invested in conspiratorial meetings and drama achieved in the confrontations and debates of public meetings. The narcissism of crises interrupts, for him, the deadly routine of teaching and the pretense of scholarship or research. He can involve his students, his colleagues, and the administration in his crises. He can become a hero or a martyr, enjoying enormous victories or suffering tremendous defeats. The vendetta pulls into its vortex all phases of life—personal friendships and enmities, promotions, appointments, schools of thought, enmity or alliance with the administration, course assignments, curricula, and the politics of the internal administration of the school. The individual takes his stand in terms of the known position of his feuding partners or of their probable response to a position he will take. He so selects his position as to be in the least unfavorable light. But if he is careful he need not worry about defeat. His tenure is his last line of defense. Thus, in an ultimate sense, he cannot be defeated, nor can he win. But he can enjoy and suffer the battle. His dependence on his feuding partners links him to a kind of ritual dance which has no outcome, only new phases and stages. At the death, retirement, resignation of his principle enemy, he discovers that he had a love-hate relationship with his enemy and mourns his departure even more than that of a friend. Certainly no friend can provide as exciting a life as that of a blood enemy.

For the work ethics the significance of the feud is that it allows suspension of all ethical norms during its course. Or rather, ethics becomes an instrument in the feud. One can practice any morally leprous act as long as the response to the act does not endanger one's own tenure. At the same time, one uses "ethics" as a rallying cry, to indicate the unethical behavior of one's enemies as they reciprocate.

Aside from the use of ethics as a device in organizational feuding, the feud overrules all other ethical considerations. As a result there are no forms of ethical leprosy that are beneath the participants of a feud. In practically no other occupational area are participants willing to stoop so low. Thus all the ethical norms we have described above become fictitious in the feud. Interpersonal relations can become a form of torture if one does not have the strength. One can become, owing to the protection of tenure, a living open sore, a social pariah, the butt of jokes, suffering indignity and humiliation. In no other institution is there as much cruelty and barbarism openly practiced as among ethically superior academic men. Business and advertising, which are cruel in the work demands they make upon their personnel, are less cruel because, through dismissal, they end the misery of defeated candidates. In the universities, the defeated need not leave, and if they stay they do so to be targets for indignity and abuse and to attempt new alliances to repay their tormentors in kind.

The above situation is not at all rare. In fact, I have observed some form of it in every school I have been able to observe in any depth. Thus the contradiction between ethical ideals or ideology and practice in the university is greater than in most institutions. But it is more than this contradiction that highlights the level of practice. The actual level of ethical practice is probably lower than in any professional organization in America.

THE ACADEMIC ENTREPRENEUR

WE HAVE INDICATED that a vast number of professors escape immurement in the university by grantsmanship. They engage in consulting for business and government, secure grants from government and foundations, and work on contract research for government agencies.

This development, at least in scope, is relatively new, having begun during and immediately after World War II. Before that time the image and the reality of the academician were that of a man who lived in an ivory tower, who never met a payroll, and who had a disinterested love for truth and pure research.

Of course, the image had its imperfections. Academicians in America traditionally had been drawn from or tied to the clergy and specialized in moral philosophy and uprightness. Some gave moral support to emergent capitalism in the nineteenth century, and a few provided moral criticism of capitalism at the same time. Occasionally a professor would be recruited and paid to write an attack on the socialists who were advocating public regulation of utilities or some other radical venture. On the whole it was felt to be morally leprous for a college professor to act as a paid publicist for industry, a trade association, or the National Association of Manufacturers. The New Deal began a period during which college professors routinely were engaged as civil servants, consultants, speech writers, or policy advisors and reviewers of government policies and practices.

Some government departments began to employ professors to write research papers, reports, and memoranda. But only during World War II did the government agencies begin to employ universities and their staffs to engage in large-scale research. Since World War II this movement has so snowballed that well over 50 percent of the budgets of some of the larger universities come from federal funds. In many, the vast majority of the staff, especially the senior staff, is not engaged in teaching or is engaged in only part-time teaching.

At the same time, the giant foundation has come into its own. The Ford Foundation was the first of a whole new group of foundations aimed at influencing and defining social policy in part through research and grants to universities and their personnel. The older foundations—the Rockefeller Foundation, the Twentieth Century Fund, the Social Science Research Council, the Carnegie Foundation, among others—began to expand their operations and to bestow larger and larger grants to universities and their staffs.

Business organizations, including advertising agencies, responding to the success of government in using academic consultants and to a new appreciation of the role of research and "science" and the value of high-prestige, disinterested names on the transmittal pages of their reports, began to employ academicians in the same way as did government agencies and foundations.

Such opportunities were totally new and unexpected by academicians. Heretofore academicians had tended to look down their noses at business and regarded themselves as too unworldly to tamper with practical affairs. The early stages of this movement resulted in a vast surge of elation and narcissism resulting from the fact that academicians could now prove they had a function. Scholars in the older tradition, however, could look down their noses on the new Philistines who "sold out" at the first nibble.

By now, however, the academic enterpriser who works on foundation grants or government contracts or grants receives high prestige and envy for his success. The consultant to private business is in a more ambiguous position. The prestige of his employment depends on what he does for whom. If he consults in the physical sciences, his employment will tend to be viewed favorably; in the social sciences, his position will be more ambiguous. If his work is viewed as "promotional" or "commercial" in purpose, he is still frowned upon. If he conducts research that is "scientific" in character, and uses techniques or models that are academic, he may save some prestige. If he is well paid for these efforts he will be both envied and resented.

With all of this, contract research and grantsmanship are a unique kind of work. Since the consultant is not directly on the payroll of a client, he has the illusion of the independence and freedom of science. He is not subject to the day-to-day discipline and supervision ordinarily a condition for salaried employment. He is expected to be treated with respect, especially since he is employed because he has unique skills that are not usually available to the organization for which he consults. Moreover, his "independence" is supposed to lend an aura of objectivity and authenticity to his findings. Because this is so, businessmen are particularly prone to employ consultants to bolster particularly vulnerable, doubtful, or shady propositions. If the work can be done without outside consultants, and if its merits are directly perceivable, the authority of the academician is unnecessary. At times, two firms, in the process of negotiations, will each employ their own captive consultants, either to neutralize each other or to prevent themselves from being led astray by the other firm's experts.

The consulting expert is usually aware of all these undercurrents. In fact he is likely to live off them. He is able to create his own market by suggesting that businessmen lack the science and know-how to run their own business. He can easily point out hundreds of areas where businesses are run in the absence of necessary facts or information, that is, purely on the basis of judgment. He can point out the vast costs of errors, opportunities missed, or mistakes which occur when one does not use science as a means of decision making. Businessmen experience a sense of their own inadequacies in the face of the superior knowledge and technique of the specialist. On his own ground the expert, unopposed by other experts, usually is unbeatable.

Having convinced the businessman that he knows nothing without science, the experienced academic consultant will outline a method or project which allegedly will solve the businessman's problem. Usually the language, the concepts, and the procedures are too involved, specialized, and scientific for the businessman to understand. Since the academician seems to know what he is talking about, and since the businessman often attributes his lack of comprehension to his own ignorance, the businessman is quite likely to buy relatively expensive but dimly understood research.

During these negotiations the academic consultant is unlikely to understand the detailed, specific *business* problem which caused the businessman to employ the consultant in the first place. The businessman may be unable to communicate the problem, because among other things these problems are less dignified than science itself. The businessman is reluctant to communicate to a dignified academician the petty, sordid, competitive details that make up much of the day-to-day routine of business.

The consultant is thus likely to embark upon an expensive, scientific study of the general class of problems that trouble the businessman instead of the specific problem. He will ask for more time and more money than are usually allowed for the solution of a specific problem, and he is given the money in the hope that the work, when done, will solve for all time not only the specific problem but also the general problem. From time to time the businessman will receive progress reports that he doesn't understand, but he will find it difficult to press the expert, because in doing so, he will reveal his own ignorance.

Finally will come the "completed" report. First of all it is incomprehensible. Moreover, making it comprehensible is hard for the businessman, because he does not know how to "get inside" the verbal and technical structure of the report in order to ask technical or intelligent questions. If he does ask questions, he finds it difficult to understand the answers. Only by risking the appearance of being dim-witted and by being persistent can he begin to understand what he has bought. It takes a man of real stature to risk appearing ignorant or stupid by asking simple, uncomplicated questions and by requiring simple, uncomplicated answers that are meaningful in terms of the business problems he faces.

If he does so, he is likely to find that while the methods employed by the "scientist" work, in general, the data available are inadequate to provide answers to the questions which the scientist agreed to solve. To complete the job another study would be necessary and cost a vast amount more than the original study. Moreover, the answer provided at a hypothetical level is an answer to a general problem and not the specific problem evoking the study. The answer is thus "academic" or philosophic but not practical. The individual businessman who argued for the study may be forced to argue for its continuance in order to justify the original decision. He may get his way because of respect for his position or because of his value to the company in other areas.

Enlightened management officials may discover that if the scientist could fool them, he can fool its customers. The scientist thus is employed to use the same techniques of science, obfuscation, and sincerity to bedazzle those customers. In this happy circumstance the scientist and the businessman engage in an informal collusion to defraud distant publics through the techniques of science.

One particular case may be instructive. A group of copywriters, engaged in developing the marketing and advertising plans for a line of school supplies, dreamed up a "better writing institute," a nonprofit foundation which would work up a program for developing scientific techniques and research to improve students' composition, spelling, and writing. Once the institute was set up, it was to be used to provide endorsements for the line of school supplies. A college president was called in as a consultant. The copywriters, though moral lepers themselves, were a little embarrassed in suggesting a "payoff" to the client. The college president embarrassed even the moral lepers by proposing endorsements, seals of approval, and scientific proof of the superiority of the school supplies, which at the time existed only as a concept. After the meeting the copywriters admitted to one another that they had finally met their master.

This example could be multiplied almost infinitely. It suggests the frequency of such actions but not the ethical norm.

Most norms, relative to the role of the academician, involve the loss of dignity by the academician in his commercial enterprise. He should not be a huckster; that is, he should not directly engage in fraudulent and undignified sales efforts. But such norms relate to publicly visible behavior of the academician. They do not involve the actual level of work. As a matter of fact many academicians enjoy "defrauding" businessmen, since businessmen are "immoral" and "stupid" anyway. They recount to one another the ways and techniques by which businessmen are misled or fall into traps and their lack of comprehension of the contracts which they sign. Moreover, the opportunity to do such consulting work provides the academician with an insight into reality, the opportunity to write articles, and, of course, an additional source of money.

In these respects academicians as consultants are usually morally inferior to all but the worst of businessmen. They initiate work with promises of results that they know in advance they cannot deliver. And they fail to deliver work they committed themselves to. As employees doing the same things, rather than as consultants, they would be fired. As consulting academicians and scientists they excuse themselves, since businessmen, being moral inferiors, are not included in the moral obligations that the academicians too frequently disregard among themselves.

In part, the problem is intrinsic to the nature of business and science. Business is based on contracts. One is expected to deliver that which is contracted for or face penalties. Science cannot guarantee results from any one endeavor since it deals with the unknown. The scientist expects failure after failure, with the vague hope of a partial success in the distant future.

When a scientist works for a businessman as a consultant,

he enters a contractual relation. Perhaps without understanding it, he is forced to promise results which as a scientist he knows he cannot expect to deliver. Since he cannot communicate the tentativeness of science to businessmen who would not understand it anyway, he enters the business relationship on the latter's terms. Doing so, however, does not guarantee the results he contracts to deliver. Scientists employed by industry (as opposed to consultants) usually develop a different approach. Since they have to live with the results of their promises, they are less likely to promise results that they cannot deliver. They are more cautious and act in this respect more like disinterested scientists than do academicians, who, because they are financially independent of the firm for whom they consult can afford to "make mistakes." They can always consult for another firm.

Of course, some scientists and nonscientists in business will make long-term promises if in the process of getting an assignment they are placed in charge of a large operation. Once in charge, they hire other scientists to do the work they now administer. If the project fails, the newly hired scientific workers are fired. The administrators are not at fault, since they did none of the work required to fulfill the promises. In addition, by the time the promises are to be redeemed, the original promisers either have moved to other firms or occupy such a high position within the original firm that they cannot be penalized for failure to deliver. Social mobility is thus achieved.

CONSULTING FOR NONPROFIT AGENCIES

GOVERNMENT AND FOUNDATION grantsmanship and subcontracting are different from consulting for business. They are more prestigious and usually observe the academic forms. But they are similar to consulting for business in that they usually involve the completion of a project, a report, a book, or an article, either of which signifies the discharge of the academic's obligation. The grant or contract is usually a promise that a certain amount of work will be done, in a specific way, which should lead to results within a given range. The higher the probability of gaining valued results, the higher the probability of gaining the grant or contract.

One can thus understand why academics are prone to be optimistic about results and to draw up proposals that seem to promise easy solutions of problems that have long troubled contractors and researchers.

Once a proposal is accepted, the academician encounters the problems of dealing with the refractory nature of the world and its resistances to neat preconceptions. The expected measurements are often unobtainable; the data are not as good as they first appeared; changes in external events upset the preconceptions of the plan; labor shortages occur and it is difficult to fill them in the contractual period; the proposal was ill thought out in terms of these contingencies. All these problems are routine in research. The scientist expects to meet them and hopes to overcome them. If he fails, the failure may be his own, or it may be intrinsic to the enterprise. But in contract research, one has committed oneself in advance to an anticipated solution. Failure not only is personal or an intrinsic feature of science, it becomes a legal failure to meet contractual obligations. To the extent that promises were knowingly made that could not be fulfilled it is also an ethical failure. Someday a congressional committee will investigate the academicians' fulfillment of their government contracts. They will have to deal with the tremendous technical complexities of dozens of highly specialized scientific fields, which no layman, not even a congressman, can understand, and with the collusion of contracting government agencies in covering up the failure of the academics they employed to do the research. They will find that professionals employed by them to investigate other professions will be unwilling to indict their professional peers and future employers.

If they succeed in cutting through the fog, they might find a national disgrace. For the norm is failure to produce promised materials and alteration of contract specifications so that a report of some sort can be delivered. Finding some way to file a report of some sort, even if it is not the promised one, is a major skill in academia, and it confers prestige. Failing at this, the academician employs a number of devices.

The most brilliant form of virtuosity is to turn each failure into the basis for another grant. Each study encounters new and unanticipated problems that must be studied before the solution to the original problem (and the report) can be issued. A new promise thus replaces the initially promised delivery, and a new grant is provided (sometimes by a new or different agency or foundation). Several more years are purchased before a report is due. In the meantime the original problem is forgotten or lost, and a succession of new problems replaces the old one. Past grants, and past failures, are evidence of expertise and qualification for new grants. For the experts can prove, on the basis of previous grants, that others trusted them. Moreover, they know more about the problems of a field than those without grant-given experience. It is thus possible, with renewals, extensions, and new sources of support, to go upward and onward for as much as ten years without issuing a final report. In the meantime the principal investigator can become a "foremost authority" on the basis of experience, anecdotes, and unpublished findings.

Such virtuosity is relatively rare. Other devices are often employed. The crudest, most common is finding another job prior to the delivery date of the contract. Doing so gets one "off the hook," but since most contract research is joint research, this device places others "on the hook." This is morally leprous unless one gets another grant or contract that is larger than the original one, in which case no one would stand in the way of the creative scientist.

The simplest way to discharge one's obligations (especially after the departure of the original senior staff) is to employ specialists in "rescue operations," skilled writers who have experience in putting together a report. These writers frequently move from project to project solving "unsolvable" problems. They have advantages over the original investigators in that they are unencumbered with the original preconceptions of the contracting parties. They can write reports that have "face validity"—so long as the original proposals are not read. Thus, skill at redefining the problem so that it fits the answers found is a major virtue.

If these methods result in a report, a physical entity, paper with words printed upon it and bound between two covers, the original contract appears to have been discharged, and the contracting party will frequently sigh with relief since his judgment of the productivity of the contractor is vindicated.

Graduate students are useful in this regard. Quite frequently they will innocently enter into the realm of a foundering project. They are often shocked that, without experience and knowledge of the areas studied, they are employed and given a "piece" of the project data to analyze and write up. Their innocence and native intelligence are their chief virtues. If, not knowing the history of the project, they pitch in and write something, even a doctoral dissertation, they enable the project to discharge its obligations. Sometimes, however, during the course of the project, they may discover the history of the project. They then begin to feel that they are exploited, because, for peanuts, they are discharging obligations which their major professors were unable to discharge. In addition, many feel that they are thrown into very narrow and specialized work at a time when they should be acquiring the broad foundations for an academic career. If they are silent and complete the task, they are well on their way to becoming professionals.

At the same time it must be recognized that a large part, I would venture to say the major part, of scholarly, controlled, large-scale research work today is being completed by students who formally are not qualified to do the job. Moreover, if this had been known in advance, the contracts and grants would not have been issued.

The principle investigator thus becomes a letterhead, someone whose name is used to sign reports and negotiate contracts. Since he is so little involved in the actual operations, he can sign many contracts. Since he is paid in terms of the amount of time he devotes to a project ($1/3$, $1/2$, or $1/27$ of his working time), use of his name involves subdivision of the self. Moreover, since use of too little time (less than 1/5) might imply inadequate supervision, the academic investigator must offer to provide substantial blocks of his time to the project. If he works on a number of projects he may be selling 200 percent, 300 percent, or even higher than 400 percent of his time. Since his sales of his "self" are made to a variety of agencies, nobody need know the extent of his self-multiplication and division. Moreover, since an individual has only 100 percent of his time to give, the transaction is only a paper one, except when the individual or his university draws multiple salaries or when the contracting agency bases its grant on the assurance that a "star" is in charge.

The only comparable case situation might be in the theater, where the producer sells more than 100 percent of the show to his backers. If the show fails, no one is the wiser. If it succeeds, the producer is embarrassed. In either case, he legally has committed fraud.

In academic contracting, there is no clear criterion of either failure or success. It is difficult to establish fraud, because no parties to the arrangement have any interest in detecting it. A relatively simple investigation could establish the fact of oversale of one's time. Many great universities draw substantial shares of their income from housing and administering grants. As a result they have a vested interest in supporting the activities of their staff members who attract funds to the university. The fraud is only an academic issue to them. They will of course be concerned when a full staff member teaches at another school, since in doing so he is scattering his seed upon the wind. They will be concerned also if he has another job for which he is paid in the form of a salary. In that case, he is moonlighting. They will be concerned also if he consults for business in an undignified way. Such an activity reflects negatively on the university. If, however, his consulting is in the form of grant-supported research, for which he brings funds, staff, and graduate students to the university, then multiple employment is salutary.

THE DISINTERESTED QUEST FOR TRUTH

THE IDEOLOGY of academic institutions rests, traditionally, on the disinterested quest for truth. No nonscientific commitment should be allowed to interfere with this quest. Academic freedom is justified on these grounds, and Communists and Catholics, at times, have not been employed because they are allegedly not free to search for the truth.

This argument, in its general form, has much merit. In fact the whole idea of science and the university is based upon it. But its implications are not always understood. Operationally, academic freedom means the freedom of the individual to define his own problems, select his techniques, and report his own findings. A judgment as to the success of a piece of scholarly work is based on criticism of it by the author's peers, and in theory, if not in fact, the whole scholarly or scientific enterprise is based on uninhibited mutual criticism. No one organizational structure is presumed to be sufficiently strong to define problems, techniques, or satisfactory results on the basis of organizational, financial, or political pressure. In essence academic freedom requires the same kinds of institutional guarantees that laissez-faire was supposed to guarantee in the economic sphere.

The tradition of academic freedom is securely held in Western society. Academicians are sensitive to all kinds of restraints on their freedom, and university administrations are most often intimidated by the fear of being denounced as academic tyrants.

But, as in most areas, lack of freedom is defined by the awareness of constraints imposed by outside bodies on the actor. It is rarely defined in terms of having independent or autonomous purposes which one wishes to actualize. Thus we are more likely to respond negatively to others who prevent us from doing what we want to do, than we are to those who prevent us from knowing what we want to do. Thus positive inducements, blandishments, and seductions are more restrictive than constraints simply because they operate beneath the level of consciousness of the individual. In ordinary parlance, this is called manipulation.

All of this is relevant, since the ideology of science and scholarship implies that the individual should be able to define his own problems, that is, should be psychologically aware of his own independence and the range of possibilities within his work. The new opportunities for prestige, promotions, and fees available to the grantee or research contractor provide positive inducements, blandishments, and seductions to work on given problems, with specified techniques, to produce a given range of results.

The individual need be aware of no external constraint unless he has a strong sense of the problems he would like to define for himself. Officially he is not called upon to alter his perspective in order to get funds. All he need do is find the funding source that is interested in his problem. He must, however, study the research announcements of the funding source, discover the criteria for grants, and write a proposal that is acceptable in the terms of the funding source. If he finds that his private interests conflict with those of the funding source he can, if he wishes, make mental reservations. He hopes to do his real work under cover of the formal proposal. However, the necessity of meeting the obligations imposed by the funding source represents an external set of pressures, to which he must give most of his time. If, in the process of doing the work, the researcher can maintain his own perspective and find the time to do his own work, he need not succumb to these other pressures. However, he risks developing a form of institutional schizophrenia brought on by the requirement of keeping his original self separate from the new self which he assumes when he undertakes the role of grantee or contractor. It is much more economical to adopt the role requirements of the grant in order not to have to fight one's work. If one does, however, one surrenders even one's psychological freedom.

In addition, undertaking contract research places upon one a set of ethical obligations to the contracting agency. One is not supposed to make it look foolish, or to indicate that some of the basic assumptions used by the agency to define the project are incorrect, especially if that agency has committed itself to those assumptions in the face of opposition. One is expected to be loyal and trustworthy. To rock the boat is a "crime." To reveal to the world the normal undersides of the world of the contractor or contracting agency is a worse crime. To be loyal and trustworthy is to adopt the bureaucratic ethic of keeping official secrets and not washing dirty linen in public.

Adopting the bureaucratic ethic means that the independent scientist is sucked into the politics and the bureaucratic world of the contracting agency. Only the nonparticipant and the institutional schizophrenic can avoid this result.

All of this does not mean that every researcher is torn by unavoidable ethical problems. On the contrary, such problems exist only where the researcher knows what it means to be independent.

For many there is no such knowledge. As the young graduate student of today enters the university he finds that many of the staff are committed to contract research and grants. The disciplines of the respective fields are shaped by the current practices, interests, and research activities of the staff. The valued scientific techniques and methodologies are most often those which produce financial support, and faculty and administration are most explicit and self-conscious about their needs. The problems selected for research are those which are fundable. A major graduate school will have dozens of "projects," and the student will be given all kinds of opportunities to "earn his way," or to be useful. It is possible for him to go through graduate school without ever coming into any significant contact with theories, techniques, and ideas that are not fundable. At times, he may hear the older theories, deriving from an era before applied research was dominant, derided and "exploded." His faith in the present is confirmed.

If the graduate student enjoys such a seamless and serene graduate training he can be fully prepared for the positive freedom of contractual research without experiencing any ethical problems. In fact he may be incapable of so doing. Only the older generations who have lived in a world that knew no contract research face the possibility of strongly experiencing these ethical quandaries. Ethical blindness rather than ethical quandaries is the fate of the younger generation who find themselves favorably situated in a modern research factory.

Fortunately or unfortunately, the seamless serenity of the graduate research factory is not perfect. Some students come to the graduate school from schools not oriented to the contract research tradition. Frequently they come in response to the great names at the school who represent an earlier tradition or who no longer practice the work upon which their outside reputation is based. When such a student becomes exposed to the narrow, technical nature of the graduate school, he frequently rebels. In some cases students educate themselves despite their professors, a remarkable feat since it requires opposition to not only their seniors but also their peers. In some schools there is an underground of discontented students whose discontent lies in the fact that their teachers are not interested in the general problems of their field but only in narrow contract research. The underground sustains the individual who rebels and permits him to continue despite the faculty.

Some students struggle to achieve autonomy because they enter graduate school with the political ideologies and ideas of their youth and of their generation. They experience narrow professional contract research as a sell-out and can thus develop an ideological defense against "academic conformism."

Others discover older traditions simply by reading books in their field which are not on prescribed reading lists. They discover for themselves (usually late in their graduate education) the classic traditions of their field as new and wonderful things. They circulate these discoveries among their friends and use them as a device to attack their professors.

Some become disenchanted with their field simply through the discovery of the senselessness of the work they do for their professors. They compare their expectations of their field with the actual work they do in it. The employment and exploitation of students serve to provide an image of much of what their professional life might be.

The experience of disenchantment with graduate schools, while general, has little chance of resulting in positive change. Only a few students have the nerve and the strength to educate themselves. The vast majority of the disenchanted drop out. A few are "dropped" out because their bad-mannered disagreements with their professors embarrass the school. They are "troublemakers."

Of those that get through, most simply accept the field as defined by their professors and never are aware of questions that might cause embarrassment. A large minority are aware of the embarrassing questions but hope to profit from the opportunities that exist by "going along." These students usually become acceptable researchers in the next generation. A small minority are aware of the limitations of their graduate education and hope to conform until they get their degree. Afterward, they tell themselves, they will do their own work. In the meantime they stuff themselves with indigestible material. By the time they get their degrees all they know is that which they formerly found intolerable. They are unequipped, because of lack of opportunity, to do that which they at one time thought would be their life work. At that later time they may discover that all they can write, teach, and use for research is what is intolerable. To continue in their field they must capitulate. Capitulation involves blinding oneself to one's original insight and, if possible, forgetting that one ever had it. These are the greatest tragedies of the operation of the academic machine. For these students it is hard even to do work within their new perspective.

Trying hard to avoid the problems caused by the young rebels and troublemakers, the advanced university screens applicants for the graduate school. Students with the wrong backgrounds or from wrong schools or interested in the wrong issues do not get admitted. Instead sane, stable, smooth, and conventional students who are interested in available projects and problems are sought after. In short, the student must brainwash himself before he enters graduate school. The professors are too busy to brainwash him.

The very same schools, however, go through anguished periods of soul searching, when they attempt to discover the reasons for the mediocrity and lack of originality of their students' doctoral dissertations. They compare the recent crop with those of their illustrious past and find that the quality of graduate students has declined. They know not why. As yet, they have not discovered the reasons. Yet a reasonable explanation could not be acceptable. For the structure of the school determines the acceptable level of reasonability of explanation. And the structure of the great graduate schools has so changed that the answers of the past no longer apply.

As a result of these processes, the problems of "ethics" are no longer ethical problems. They are problems of social structure, and as every good sociologist knows, problems of social structure are problems of fact and not of ethics. The new graduate schools are well on their way to solving the problems of ethics. They have done so simply by abolishing them. As a result, the system may be corrupt in its entirety with everybody in it, except for the unhappy few, being able to act in an ethically acceptable way. Ethics, or the lack of ethical sensibility, becomes an objective fact, removed from individual awareness or concern.

The ideology of disinterested science thus becomes an organization tool which allows its practitioners to sell their science while being free from any constraints imposed upon them by the ideology. This is the best of all possible worlds if one has developed the personal psychology to go along with it. Most of us have.

THE ETHICS OF WELFARE WORKERS

IT IS DIFFICULT to describe the operative ethical norms among social workers, since much of the work is done "in the field" and therefore is inaccessible to an outside observer. Reports of efforts among social and welfare workers of their own and others' experience must suffice.

When observed in one's work, all the extremes in the typical pattern of adjustment, outlined on pages 97 to 101, become the source of moral disapprobation by others. These extremes include:

1. *Sadism and abuse of the client.* The social or welfare worker may from the standpoint of middle-class morality punish the client to an extreme degree for failing to have middle-class virtues. If he reports punitive action to another worker he is likely to be regarded as a moral leper. Enjoyment of such abuse is even more despised.

2. *Playing God.* This applies especially if it involves a cruel and unusual punishment or penalty. It is viewed as a moral defect. Making crucial decisions that negatively affect the life of the client, without attempting to gather the ascertainable facts, is a serious moral lapse. Accepting such responsibilities without protest is equally "immoral." Both such strictures are unlikely to affect the sincere believer in his own godhead, since he solves his own problems by possessing a sense of certainty.

3. *Failure to maintain minimal contact with the client.* Here one must be careful in making judgments. Welfare and social workers arc too often overworked with large case loads and much paper work to be able to see all their clients. Most keep track of the client by telephone or by completing less than the number of specified home visits. They usually are forced to fake reports of such visits. However, there are standards among workers of the amount of "goofing off" and the amount of faking of records that are permissible. Exceeding these limits is morally leprous.

4. "Shaking down" a client for a share of the loot or exploiting a female client sexually. There are very few cases of these, and they are the most serious offenses, on which there is complete unanimity of censure.

Surrounding all these norms is a psychological identification with the client. The client must be protected against the sadism, megalomania, laziness, and psychopathy of the social worker who develops these traits. In part the traits are accentuated by both the complete powerlessness of the client with respect to the welfare worker and by the client's low social position. Welfare and social work thus can allow for the development of latent pathologies in the worker, pathologies which in other jobs would be checked by their very inability to be expressed without punishment. The ethical norms of the social and welfare workers are defenses against their own worst natures.

The identification with the client springs, in addition, from the ideology of social work itself. The welfare and social worker is there to protect the otherwise unprotected. But the ideology comes into conflict with other ideologies. The ideology of the taxpayer and the elected official, in part, is to keep costs down and to make receiving welfare unattractive as a way of life. The welfare administrator is thus hemmed in by budgets which result in narrow rules regarding eligibility for benefits, and by payments to the client which are usually below the minimum requirements for health. These are administered through innumerable forms, rules, and procedures, all of which force the welfare worker to justify every expenditure. The rules, procedures, and forms thus strain the resources of the welfare worker who identifies with the client.

The knowledgeable welfare worker thus learns how to break the rules, to lie, to cheat, to forge or destroy documents in the interest of the client. To do this within reasonable bounds is not considered unethical by the workers themselves, but it does cause problems for supervisors. Supervisors or would-be supervisors who wish to make a career out of welfare administration must identify with the rules. If they wish to advance in the welfare bureaucracy they are forced to be legalistic, respectful of the world of paper, and punitive of the client. If they go beyond what is necessary for promotion they are viewed as moral lepers.

Much of the casework in public welfare is done by graduate students and by young men and women with college degrees who have trained for no other profession. They look upon welfare work as a temporary job until they can select a career, or "find themselves." Since they do not expect to remain in welfare work, they cannot readily identify with the restrictive rules, procedures, and punitive philosophy they

find in welfare. They would prefer to be more closely linked
to their clients than their bosses would like them to be. There
is thus a continual tug-of-war between worker and supervisor
over the issue of leniency and liberality in benefits and procedures. The problem is compounded by the career lines of the
supervisor. Since a professional career in public welfare is
relatively low paying and low in prestige, it attracts many
individuals from the "lower classes." This is only to say that a
low-paying, low-prestige, and intrinsically unsatisfying job is
attractive to those whose alternatives are even worse jobs. But
to the "lower-class" official who has reached middle-class
status through a career in social work, the job is not unsatisfying. Because it has brought him respectability, status, and
ascent he identifies with his job, and with its appurtenances
or "scenery"—forms, procedures, and verbiage that confirm
his status. Moreover, since he regards his ascent as a personal
triumph over social circumstances, he is likely not to feel
sympathetic to those who did not have the moral fiber to
overcome their lower-class background. The successful supervisor from a lower-class background is thus not likely to be
sympathetic to his caseworkers or clients. He, moreover, has
a professional and personal interest in the inviolability of the
correct filling out of forms and procedures. His subordinates,
especially college graduates of middle-class parentage, take the
opposite stance. As a result there is a duel between caseworker and supervisor, with the supervisor being inclined to
punish the class from which he came.

The supervisor, above all, is interested in procedural correctness and in keeping his skirts administratively clean. He
will tolerate leniency upon the part of his subordinates if
there is not a clear violation of the law and if the violations
are carried out in such a way as not to implicate him. Workers and supervisors thus work out complicated verbal formulae by which, through totally indirect means, the worker
can communicate to the supervisor that he managed to take
such steps that are necessary to increase a family allowance
without providing a clear violation of the law. He may have
forged a document or escalated a client's weight to over 250
pounds so that the client may get special clothing allowances.

He may have found a suggested roominghouse unsatisfactory so that the client can stay in a hotel or in her own familiar neighborhood. The ethical rule in such situations is for the welfare worker to use the secret language of his profession. He should never admit to his supervisor a gross illegality, since to do so would make the supervisor an accomplice and force him to become excessively strict in order not to be involved. Thus the ethical norm involves maintaining the fiction of legality when in fact the actions are illegal. In actual operation then, the ethics of illegality supersede the ethics of legality.

Such an arrangement is a compromise. It allows the supervisor to maintain his respect for the rules, and the welfare worker to retain his identification with the client. By using Aesopian language they can continue a working arrangement with each other, yet maintain their differences. The ethics of illegality works to prevent an intolerable situation from becoming manifest. It works, and is perhaps the best possible compromise, in the absence of changes in punitive rules or procedures or of changes which might overcome the basic opposition between supervisor and welfare worker.

The identification of the welfare worker with the client causes interesting complications in his relationship with the client. The welfare worker undertakes all kinds of illegal activities to secure aid for the client. He may lie, falsify records, fail to report significant data, or even forge the client's name to documents. In many cases the client may be unaware of the subterfuges and illegalities committed in his interests. He may embarrass the welfare worker by inadvertently or consciously providing information to others that exposes these subterfuges and illegalities. If he does this the welfare worker is in trouble. Therefore, the welfare worker wants the client to be totally truthful with him. He wants the client to indicate unreported sources of income, the existence of a common-law husband, or other data that affect the worker's reports. Thus while the worker reserves the right to use illegality with respect to his own boss, he demands truthfulness from his subordinates. If the client "louses" him up, by telling him lies which might embarrass him or cause him extra work, he is likely to become punitive toward the client.

In short, the welfare worker is likely to develop toward his clients a paternalistic attitude which reduces them to the role of children. The welfare worker will, of course, argue that they are children.

THE ETHICS OF THE PROFESSIONAL SOCIAL WORKER

THE ETHICAL PROBLEMS that professional social workers face differ from those of welfare workers. As the work of either relates to indigent or lower-class clients, however, they share many of the same problems.

Professional social workers become involved with the courts in problems related to divorce, the custody of children, delinquency, and the commitment of family members to mental institutions. Their professional status makes it easier for them than for welfare workers to adopt megalomanic attitudes and decisions. Social workers are, of course, experts, and many of them feel entitled to make vital decisions concerning their clients, without undertaking a thorough investigation of the case and without awareness of the uncertainties in predicting the outcome of their actions. A great many professional social workers would like to make the practice of social work a state-certified profession. One purpose, and not by far the principal purpose, is to make the conversation and interview with the client privileged information. Thus a social worker's *opinions* would not become the legal basis for drastic actions by courts or other judicial or administrative agencies.

One ethical norm which is invoked (rather infrequently) involves the use of clients in experimental problems. In some cases clients and students will be used to demonstrate a technique, such as group therapy, group dynamics, or perhaps psychotherapy. The amount of treatment or therapy is usually sufficient to demonstrate the techniques but not to complete the treatment. In some cases partial treatment may be worse than no treatment at all. Group therapy that involves a fixed number of sessions (to fit into an academic term, for instance) may terminate at exactly that point at which a large number of clients are particularly vulnerable, aggressive, or defensive. In terminating the sessions at such a point, the social worker or psychologist may seriously damage his patients or students even though he fulfills his academic assignment as a teacher.

The use of patients in psychodrama or sociodramas for one session is valuable in disseminating the technique to potential practitioners. It is less valuable for the subjects.

In the same way, professional social work supervisors may practice on their staffs. Using the armory of psychological techniques, the experienced professional may attack the motives, personality, and self-image of the subordinate. This is done under the guise of making the subordinate aware of his motivations and biases. But when used by a superior with regard to a subordinate in "normal" social relations, manipulative techniques have much more than educational meanings and consequences. The subordinate cannot defend himself, as can a client or patient, since, if he wins the argument, he might lose his job. As a result the sadistic supervisor or "the pathogenic boss" has a license to use the techniques of therapy to attack, control, and manipulate his subordinates. He can force them to leave, to become dependent upon him, or to experience severe loss of feelings of self-esteem or other personality disturbances. The use of psychological techniques as techniques of one-upmanship, or as techniques of bureaucratic and personal warfare, has been commented upon by novelists, primarily with respect to interpersonal relationships among psychiatrists. Its use in bureaucratic settings has been little discussed. In professional social work, the abuse of such techniques is not infrequent, and the use of them by an experienced supervisor on less experienced subordinates is viewed as a form of moral leprosy.

Professional social workers are likely to be more sensitive than other professionals or businessmen to the use of professional ideologies as a technique for advancing the career. In part they are sensitive to moral lapses because their professional and personalized ideologies involve strong elements of an egalitarian and democratic tradition. They use and believe the language of democracy and of the sacredness of personality. The language becomes part of their second nature. It becomes a rationale for many of their actions, whether or not they are democratic or humanitarian. The ideology serves as a cover for organizations which are essentially and necessarily not democratic.

Yet they expect them to be so. Thus they are more critical of their bosses than are other professionals when their bosses lie to them, go behind their back, or use techniques of manipulation that are intrinsic to the authority of a boss. At the same time, their bosses provoke condemnation since they rarely present issues in terms of necessity, power, or economic realities. The attraction to ideology means that all expediencies are dressed up in ideological form, though the disguises are all too often clumsy and transparent. Nevertheless, the subordinate is expected to accept expedient decisions on ideological grounds. He must brainwash himself even if the ideological disguise is transparent and operates against his own self-interest. It is not surprising that most social workers think that their bosses are hypocrites, sell-outs, and moral lepers.

The "opportunity to be democratic" occurs in those agencies that live off grants from private foundations or public institutions. The opportunity to be democratic consists in endless staff conferences. The professional staff of the agency, including consultants being paid ten dollars to twenty-five dollars an hour, can spend a substantial part of its collective time on the job reviewing case after case for no apparent purpose other than to educate each other and the directors. Procedures are reviewed, and a "collective conscience" is developed, though all parties to the conference except the directors privately resent the waste in time and money. Such conferences serve, however, to use up the budget and provide the basis for new budgets. In a similar manner vast expenditures are made in typing up of protocols of therapy sessions, minutes of conferences, and handbooks of operations and procedures.

The same personnel may also be involved in private practice. A private "nonprofit" agency will serve as a recruiting ground for patients for their private practice. The social worker, therapist, or psychologist in a social work agency may serve as a part-time therapist on the staff of this private agency and treat patients or conduct group therapy at a much lower hourly rate than charged for private practice. In the course of such therapy they "graduate" clients to their more lucrative private practice.

In the private "nonprofit" clinic, care is devoted in intake and assignment procedures to distribute the most prosperous clients fairly among the staff. It is considered unethical to arrange to monopolize those patients who are potentially the most available, that is, prosperous, for private practice.

Since such a clinic serves primarily as a recruiting ground for private patients, all time spent not seeing patients is regarded as wasted. As a result there are few staff meetings, records are kept in longhand, and procedures are simple. The cost of treatment per patient may be from one-third to one-tenth of that of an agency that operates on a grant.

The problem that remains is to decide which type is less ethical. One, by emphasizing the dignity of the conference, makes it difficult to treat all but a few patients; the other is far more efficient. But the hope of recruiting private patients is a major cause of the efficiency. In the long run, perhaps the patients are exploited if they are directed to forms of therapy that are more expensive than necessary.

Yet this emphasis on ethical issues beclouds other basic issues in social work. Many, I would guess most, social workers are concerned with the lack of facilities and resources to treat their clients or patients, and with their lack of knowledge and the techniques to do so. They are also concerned with the fact that fundamental causes of the symptoms that evoke the need for social work lie outside the field itself. In a larger sense, they are concerned with the structure of a society that permits ignorance, poverty, disease, and pathology to be a fundamental part of that society. They do not know the answer to these problems, but their sensitivity to them betrays a genuine moral sensibility that is only partly a product of their job. They attempt to live within the framework of their ideology, and this is one of the most difficult tasks of all to perform. Most social workers compare favorably with other professionals.

THE ETHICS OF POVERTY
PROGRAMMING

IN MOST of our discussion of occupational ethics we have attempted to define ethical norms by the actions related to work which evoke responses of disapproval, horror, or disgust from one's colleagues. The ethical norms or standards are defined by the response of others to the violation of the norms or standards. Such a procedure presupposes the existence of norms or standards, and the only problem in the study of ethical norms is one of locating the norms. However, this procedure will not work in a stituation where there are no ethical standards or where there is no agreement over the substance of norms. To a large extent this is true of the case of community action poverty programs.

Only one case of the expression of genuine moral indignation was observed in a year of the poverty program described earlier. In this case, a community action programmer overheard two other staff members discussing behind closed doors the state of work in the organization and the mess they were in. She complained bitterly at the next staff meeting that people were talking about her behind her back, and this was unethical. How she overheard through closed doors was never explained.

There were no other ethical issues per se. Instead there were ideological issues that transcend the problems of ethics in the narrow sense of the word. From my knowledge of certain of these programs I found that many staff members had a personal or group-defined ideology which became their standard of judgment for the entire project. The ideology had two aspects. The first consisted of a racial ideology, and the second consisted of a definition of the tactics by which the racial ideology should be accomplished.

The racial ideology consists in the fact that Negroes have been the victims of exploitation, segregation, discrimination, ghettoization, and degradation. The purpose of the community action program was to reverse these white-imposed sources of degradation. The basic conflicts among the staff concerned the extent to which the white "power structure" was to be defined as the source of the community's problems, and the extent to which the purpose of the program was to attack the white power structure.

Two members on the staff of one program, who could be described as Black Nationalists and the Neo-Castroite new-leftist members felt that their function was to activate the community, to preach antiwhite propaganda to organize rent strikes, to participate in anti-board of education strikes, to demonstrate otherwise, and to preach revolution if necessary.

The "professionals" on the staff also shared at times in the anti-white power structure ideology. But their focus was narrower. They felt that it was necessary to create community-wide public opinion to ensure financial support of the project. Creation of community-wide opinion would result in putting political pressure on city hall to prevent the city from absorbing the project into its own "power structure." The civil rights movement and the existence of anti-white civil rights groups had created a climate in the Negro community that meant that no Negro leader or organization could aspire to leadership without attacking the white power structure. Thus all Negro leaders, regardless of their degree of militancy, are forced because of their competition with other leaders to express militancy and attacks on the "discriminators."

The attack on the white power structure, moreover, represents a conscious technique to evoke the guilt of white liberals and politicians. The attacks are thus directly strategic in fund raising. In addition the attacks almost always convey the implication that if the funds deserved are not made available, a race riot might ensue. Good technique suggests this will happen as a result of failure to support the community action program because the potential rioters, the community, are so enthusiastic about the program that failure to finance it will be considered an insult to the community. To suggest that the community action group will stimulate or encourage a riot is, of course, viewed as a failure in tactics, since such a threat causes the "white power structure" to view the organization with alarm.

Also, the militant tone, at a later date, protects the organization from charges of waste, inefficiency, fraud, dishonesty, and incompetence, since all such charges obviously must come from white racists, who by their charges are denying the ghetto community its opportunity to achieve equality.

With all these elements of agreement, there seems to be little room for ideological disagreements, but ways are found to disagree.

A central issue is the extent to which a community action program undertakes ameliorative, remedial, or even preventive social or psychological services. To the ideologists, all actions aimed at remedying specific defects among the population of the ghetto are means of either buying off the community, wiping up a mess after the damage has been done, or inducing the victims of exploitations to settle for an inferior position.

Thus work programs are viewed as means by which Negro youths are induced for low pay to accept low-grade jobs that perpetuate their inferior position. Educational programs are viewed as devices by which Negro youths are induced to accept white middle-class standards. Recreational arts and crafts programs are considered to be forms of "bread and circuses," which divert youth from their true purposes of achieving economic and political equality or dominance.

In addition the ideologist believes that the whole community action program is a "deal" created by the white power structure to "buy off" community leaders who are members of the black bourgeoisie and willing tools of the whites. The board of directors and the executive director are charged with being selected for their positions because they are willing to accommodate themselves to the white power structure, in exchange for which they are given jobs, sops to their vanity, and leadership over the ghetto community. Even the expressions of militancy by the community leaders are viewed as fraudulent, since the leaders to some ideologists appear as if they are concerned with only their own jobs, their budgets, and programs that are short of revolution. In short there is nothing that the community leaders and executive directors can do short of advocating revolution, that would satisfy the ideologists.

From the standpoint of the executive director and the staff, the ideologists are totally irresponsible. If not watched, they might endanger the entire project. They can do this by involving it in unauthorized demonstrations, by making untimely statements, and by creating false impressions of the project. By attempting to develop a community public opinion to which their superiors must respond, they will try to force the project to go in the direction they would push it.

In addition the ideologists write reports and memoranda which from the point of the executive director are inflammatory and provocative. Since some of these reports and memoranda are addressed to the white "power structure," that is, foundations and governmental funding agencies, the executive director can never be sure that the ideologists do not want the project to fail. In that case their ideologies would appear to be right: "One can expect no real program or action to come from an organization financed by whites." Certainly the repeated exposure of the organization to unnecessary risks is dangerous whether these risks are the results of design or obsession.

These ideological differences provide, in part, the framework of the discussion of ethics. The extreme positions taken by the ideologist constitute disloyalty, in the eyes of the professional; and the "pragmatism" or lily-livered accommodations of the professionals constitute betrayal to the ideologist. Each is unethical in the other's eyes. But each has ideological grounds for justifying his actions with respect to the other and to the organization on grounds that their ideologies are higher in value than the stated purposes of the organization. As a result neither can be forced to be ethically responsible to the other.

The actions that spring from these approaches are manifold.

Every organization that attempts to create and achieve an organizational integrity expects that certain internal discussions, conflicts, weaknesses, and malfeasances are kept secret, that is, are not revealed to outsiders. This is sometimes called the ethic of bureaucratic secrecy and sometimes the ethic of not washing dirty linen in public.

Virtually every member of the staff of the community action project had a constituency outside the organization. In some cases this constituency included rival organizations who were allegedly competing for the same funds as was one community action program. In some cases the constituency was a political group that was opposed to the community action program. In other cases it was the press, and different members of the organization had special contacts with "local political leaders" in both parties and at various levels and some had "pipelines" into city hall. Others had special connections with various government departments whose jurisdictions cut across those of the community action program.

Where these alliances and liaisons were of permanent nature, the project staff kept a steady flow of confidential memoranda, information, and written and unwritten reports going into the rival, enemy, or competing agency. In some cases city hall received copies of memoranda addressed to city hall, before the final drafts were typed and distributed. Sent to city hall were reports of discussions designed to combat city hall and copies of minutes of the executive meetings. City hall obligingly warned the executive director of the disloyalty of his staff. At one point the executive director began to hold meetings outside his office and left his notes untyped in order to prevent leaks. One member of the executive board was dropped from the board because he continually reported the results of executive board meetings to his departmental superiors in a competing organization, even before any action was taken. In one case a board member called a meeting of all local politicians to protest the imperialistic designs of the community action organization on his own organization. In this case, the board member was perhaps only protecting his occupational interest.

Damaging and harmful information that only was accessible to staff members somehow found its way into the press. These leaks occurred only at time of crises.

At least five different competing agencies were aware of secret information which should have been known only to the operations of the agency by the staff and executive board. Allegedly unfavorable reports of the activities of the executive director were presented to the executive board by the staff via informal channels. A number of crises were precipitated in this way.

Certain members of the secretarial and administrative staff were either fired or forced to resign because they allegedly leaked information to former bosses who had earlier left the project.

Not all these violations of what are normally called ethical standards had ideological bases. At least four staff members who leaked information to rival or competing organizations did this in the expressed hope that they would get a job from the competing organization if and when the community action organization failed in its attempts to get funded. The staff members included the ideologists who opposed the organization on principle. All the board members who leaked information did so apparently in terms of expediency.

Violations of the ethic of bureaucratic secrecy was only one type of violation of an ethical norm. In other cases the violation was related to information blockages. In such cases the staff member would not relay a piece of necessary information to another staff member relative to the latter's job. Such behavior always resulted in protests, since both in reality and in fantasy the lack of information justified the inability of the bypassed person to do his job. Beyond this, one of the key executives charged a secretary, at the request of her boy friend, of destroying documents before they reached the director so that he would not have access to vital information. We cannot judge if the charge is true. It is true that vital documents were frequently missing. It is also true that the executive director frequently found later that he had misfiled the missing documents. Certainly the atmosphere of the organization could evoke latent attitudes of paranoia.

Another form of violation of informational norms was provided in the phenomenon of "squealing." Ordinarily it is considered unethical for a boss to induce subordinates to "squeal" on one another. Moreover, in an organization in which the vast majority of the staff opposed the successive executive directors, one might not expect much squealing. But this was not the case. The philosophy of the second executive director was that withholding information was a sign of immaturity. Since staff members were grown up they were obligated to inform on one another. In one case a staff member was forced to resign because he would not provide the names of subordinates who had protested to him against organizational policies. By and large, there was little protest by staff against informing. The executive director would promptly reprimand a malefactor for any action he had committed immediately after the informer's report of the act. As a result, the informing stopped.

Other ethical "lapses" were not ideological in nature. A board member and a consultant did not consider it unethical to submit proposals to the board to fund their own or their wife's private organizations. Nor did they consider it unethical to employ relatives, or sons of friends, regardless of qualification or of standard employment procedures. With respect to program operation one could conclude that, after the ideologists were dismissed, there were almost no standards other than success in obtaining funding. Glowing, optimistic reports of fouled-up, nonexistent, or mismanaged programs were a matter of course. The collective attempt to conceal the actual state of program operations involved a high degree of cooperation and enthusiasm among the newer administrative staff. Research was designed to produce these optimistic results, and all research that reflected the reality was ruthlessly repressed. Reporters of the underlying reality were dismissed as having negativistic, un-American and antiauthority attitudes. If the reporters were white they were labeled racists; if they were not, they were considered to be emotionally disturbed. The direct suppression of inconvenient facts and the issuance of roseate press releases were more blatant in this program than any I have ever seen in any other kind of business organization. Yet they were justified on the grounds that the organization was surrounded by enemies. Any evidence of malfunctioning of the program would be used by enemies to kill the program, and therefore such evidence rightfully should be suppressed. The reasoning was probably correct, since many of the researchers, after seeing it in operation, were totally disenchanted by the program. They were active in their opposition because of what they thought was obvious mismanagement of the program; because they felt that the program was designed to do nothing but to use up a budget; and because the pressures placed upon them not to do their job of program evaluation or to falsify their results were so great that these pressures alerted them to the need for falsification.

The young researchers on their own part did not appreciate that much of the obvious mismanagement was due to the haste in getting a program started with only ten days' lead time. Moreover, the attitude of ideological sanctity of the researchers caused them to regard themselves as above and beyond the organization in acting as judges of the organization and the conscience of the poor.

In short, a great part of the pressure to create a Potemkin Village out of a hurriedly conceived poverty program was due to enforced haste and personal and organizational insecurity, enhancing an almost paranoiac feeling that the world was conspiring to destroy the project. The paranoiac feeling could be considered only partly pathological since in substance the reality supported the feeling.

To ensure the success of the program, some critics were hired as consultants and therefore silenced. Others were hired as staff members, and still others were silenced by promises of jobs that never came through.

While all this was going on, glowing press releases were

issued, and carefully constructed guided tours were arranged for visiting dignitaries to give the program an aura of activity, optimism, and enthusiasm. By and large public relations were the most successful operation of the project.

In one respect the project appeared to be outstanding. Because of the experience of other poverty projects, tight fiscal controls were set up. All funds were rigidly accounted for, and all expenditures required precise and exact authorization and accountability. This in part was due to the employment of a highly able comptroller, who was instructed to allow no trace of financial scandal to touch the organization. The procedures were highly successful, though at times the cost of the time spent obtaining authorization for an expenditure was greater than the expenditure. At other times, the operation of the program was delayed for weeks because authorization for the purchase of necessary supplies took so long.

Because of these activities there were none of the financial scandals so typical of many poverty programs. Yet in its design, the tight fiscal control was conceived of as a form of public relations of more importance than program operation.

All the above description deals with the *quality* of behavior in the organization. It presents no picture of the quantity of "unethical" behavior. Yet, because of the absence of clear-cut ethical norms within the organization it is difficult to call unethical much of the behavior so designated here. In fact the absence of such norms was one of the most distinctive apsects of the organization. The extent to which the behavior described here as unethical can legitimately be so called depends upon our violating our own definition of ethics. There can be no unethical behavior where there are no ethical standards. If, however, we use as a definition of ethics the standards that function in advertising, we would at least be able to make some comparison.

In our discussion of advertising we used the concept of the moral leper as a means of defining the ethical norms of the conduct of agency personnel. The moral leper is a person who by the extent of his capacity to evoke responses of horror in others tells the others what their standards are. In this respect he is a valuable person. I can safely say that in my ten years of experience in advertising I met three persons who consistently exhibited a wide range of behavior that would be called morally leprous. Such individuals personified the concept. Technically they might have been called psychopaths except that at times they were useful to their organization. Another two or three persons developed strong symptoms of moral leprosy under periods of extreme pressure but returned to "normal" when the pressure lifted. A large number of other persons sporadically showed one or more traits of moral leprosy.

The three moral lepers and the two or three pressure-prone moral lepers represent a very small percentage of all the persons I had an opportunity to observe during the ten years I spent in advertising. I would estimate that these constituted much less than one percent of the individuals I was able to observe. In the community action program the number of individuals who exhibited multifaceted symptoms of extreme moral leprosy (by advertising standards) was at least 60 percent of those whom I had the opportunity to observe. Of course, such comparisions may be unfair. All the "moral lepers" in the community action program had high-minded ideological reasons to justify their actions. Moreover, all these staff members were working in a totally new occupational area, in a new organization for which no norms had been developed. Therefore their actions were not governed by a kind of public morality that had crystallized over time and through usage. In addition, the growth of the new area of poverty programming created vast new opportunities for individuals who had previously not been exposed to such opportunities in a program that could equally succeed or fail. The desperation to succeed could thus induce pressures to act in ways singular even in comparison to advertising. Advertising has developed norms, and unwillingness or inability to comply with them can cause personal failure.

The lack of ethical standards is not unique to the particular program described here. The author believes that the com-

munity action program herein described does not reflect the
extremes to which many poverty programs have descended.
Its staff was more qualified than most, and the internal pressures were less severe than in most. As a result, individuals
were forced to less extreme forms of behavior than in most
poverty programs.

After all, the community action program did get organized,
did conduct programs, and did achieve some degree of financial responsibility. A history of other poverty programs would
reveal all the types of behavior herein described plus the
financial mismanagement, total incompetence, and political
obstinacy and deadlocks that prevent a vast number of such
programs from "getting off the ground." It is the ability to
survive that constitutes a major test of a new program. In this
respect the program was successful. It survived. The quality
of its survival is as much related to what it does in the future
as it is to its hurried and overpressured past.

For all these reasons, it is perhaps understandable that
ethical behavior in any poverty program is at the level described. Given several years of operation, poverty programs
might well develop norms that become binding upon their
members. Moreover, the process of hiring and firing and of
investigation and punishment will undoubtedly result in professional staffs that meet the standards at least of academia, if
not those of social work or advertising. Once the poverty
programs routinize their operation many of the glaring violations of public and private ethical norms may disappear.

The creation of norms, that is, the suppression of "ab-
normal" behavior, can be genuine or spurious. If it is spurious, the directors of the programs will learn the techniques of
concealing that internal mismanagement which is offensive
when exposed. If this is accomplished, poverty organization
may become not unlike many higher-type organizations in
government, business, academia, or philanthropy. Their public ideology will not be violated by any public appearance of
its opposite. If the creation of norms is to be more than a
public relations device, they must develop genuine programs
that can help the poor. These programs must be well managed by staffs that can acquire the knowledge, training, and

experience to carry out the programs. In this sense, the development of ethical norms is much more than a problem in ethics: it depends on the ability of an organization and its personnel to do their job without recourse to the many forms of fraud that constitute the violation of recognized ethical standards.

PART IV

*

*A Comparative Note
on the Meaning of Work in Its Personal
and Social Settings*

ETHICS AND SOCIAL STRUCTURE

OUR STUDY of these occupations leaves us with some feeling that the conditions under which people work in them and their behavior at work do not make in any large measure for self-realization, satisfaction, or elementary psychological or mental health. This impression may be due in part to the nature of these particular occupations. Certainly they do not constitute a cross section of all occupations. The advertising man is not representative of all businessmen in general, and especially not of the skilled professionals in business like engineers, chemists, and accountants, whose work is related to producing a tangible product by using techniques whose application leads to objectively measurable results. Rather, advertising represents an extreme form of a business-oriented occupation. Its high-risk and high-reward potential, and the impracticability of objectively measuring individual or group contributions are characteristic of much work in the middle and upper reaches in business and government; but in few areas, except perhaps politics, the theater, and the mass media, do these conditions obtain to the same degree.

The nonprofit areas herein described may also be atypical. Certainly the poverty program as an occupational setting represents an extreme case of the creation of a new occupation. As such it may be revealing. The academic occupations represent an institution unique in Western society, comparable in the past only to the ministry in the halo of ideological legitimacy they enjoy. Academia is a world that celebrates creativity and protects its celebrants. Yet it is substantially different from the arts, which offer less financial protection to the creator and more risk of failure, and reward the creator only for work done, if at all.

The new atmosphere of grants, philanthropic support, government subsidies, and academic positions for creative artists makes artistic work increasingly similar to academic work, especially as the latter becomes subject to the same influences. And yet the painter, the independent writer, the performing musician, all live in worlds different from that of the academicians.

Our analysis does not cover such professions as medicine, the law, and those others whose practitioners may be largely self-employed; Even when not so, these professions have vast opportunities for identification with their occupation, because their success and self-esteem are intimately identified with their own work rather than that of a bureaucracy they serve.

Social work is similar in many ways to much civil service work, in which an ideology of service combines with the bureaucratic organization of work. Yet because of its high ideals and the confrontation of those ideals with the most intractable reality, social work is different from much civil service work, where the "office" rather than the field is the focus of work.

We have overlooked the work of the farmer and skilled and unskilled laborer, the small businessman, and the low-skilled and semiskilled service occupations. These we point out are the limitations of our study.

Yet our study points to a number of general problems related to most occupations in our society. Some of these problems relate to: (1) the nature, locus, and level of ethics within an occupation and the focus of those ethics on the behavior of individuals as members of an in-group or on their relationship with outsiders or the society at large; (2) the role of ideologies in the formulation of occupational ethics and in providing meanings for work; (3) the level of autonomy and bureaucratization of work and its effect on the meaningfulness of work; (4) the relationship of work to deeper levels of the personality of the individual.

Our study may enable us to comment on these issues. The wide range in the fields covered provides the basis for a number of continua which express the situations not only of the fields themselves but a vast variety of other occupations.

COMPARATIVE ETHICS

OCCUPATIONAL ETHICS can be conceived of as norms that govern relationships first, among the members of an occupational field and second, between the members of the field and outsiders.

If this distinction is applied to the occupations we have described, we find a vast range of behavior in both categories.

ADVERTISING

IN ADVERTISING there are highly defined ethical norms that operate internally. This code sometimes goes so far as to include the client. Thus needless exploitation, deceit, and manipulation are frowned upon, and in blatant forms evoke disgust. At the same time, the rule *"caveat emptor"* is the principle governing relations with the public. So far as I know, there is no level of deceit, misinformation, or manipulation that advertising men would not bend to to help sell their clients' products; and although a few agencies decline to accept liquor or cigarette advertising, they do so more often on economic grounds than on ethical ones. This does not mean that all advertising is dishonest and deceitful. At times, honesty pays. A totally fraudulent claim may be disproved in such an obvious way that exposure reflects negatively on sales. An FTC cease-and-desist order may likewise produce "negative advertising." As a result, advertising agencies, under protest, will often produce copy that literally complies with the requirements of the FTC and will attempt to develop products whose advertising reflects the requirements of the Pure Food and Drug acts and the Department of Agriculture. They will carefully write copy that suggests a vast range of benefits without ever claiming benefits that are not demonstrable. Thus it is governmental rulings and public opinion that make advertising as honest as it is. Ethics are irrelevant in this area. Law then replaces personal ethics as a guarantee of minimally decent behavior. Only a few manufacturers and their agencies are willing to take a chance on obviously illegal advertising or obviously illegal products, in the hope of not being caught, or in the hope that sufficient profits will justify the fraud before governmental action suspends the illegal marketing. Companies that do so are usually small companies that have little to lose and much to gain by fraud. Larger companies, with vast capital investments, heavy costs, and expensive, established "public images" are less likely to risk the losses that may result from bad publicity. When the criteria for legally acceptable advertising are clear-cut, agencies and their clients attempt to comply. They may attempt to overstate their product's claims as much as possible, risking a cease-and-desist order, when the criteria are vague. Thus it is more the uncertainty of legal prohibitions than their severity that poses a problem for the advertiser and the agency. This, of course, does not prevent copywriters, agency officials, and advertisers from complaining about the "dictators" in Washington, especially if sales of an inferior product are declining.

Yet, with all of this, it is law, not ethics, that governs these external relations, and a well-administered but severe law will work to protect the public, despite the lack of ethics of the advertising man.

We have indicated that there are relatively strong and high standards of interpersonal ethics in advertising. We have attempted to explain these by citing the absence of any other means of justifying one's actions except personal acceptance of the informal norms. Advertising has no strong ideology which allows the individual to sacrifice everyone else for the cause. Moreover, the pressures in advertising are so intense that the agency could easily become much worse than it is, that is, could destroy itself, as a result of personal and clique warfare, a phenomenon that occasionally occurs. Thus personal ethics appear to be a response to the dangers of overaccepting the pressures and opportunities in the field. By limiting one's own exploitation of others to those actions that are necessary for survival, the members of the agency assure one another that an occupational life is possible despite the pressures. Advertising men are constantly aware of pressures. In recognizing them, they attempt to limit them. The limitations become the basis of ethics. In short, advertising men enact a "social contract" to let one another live and thus guarantee the possibility of their own occupational existence. Since this is done in the absence of strong ideologies, it represents a minimal but naturalistic basis for social life. It is a genuine social contract.

ACADEMIC ETHICS

IF ADVERTISING represents a field with high levels of internal ethics and low levels of external ethics, then academia represents the opposite. The traditions of the past, the ideology of the disinterested search for truth, and the educational, intellectual, and cultural improvement of society are continuously reinforced by the public relations of the university and of the scholar as well as by the scholar's trade associations or professional societies. His claims are reinforced by a vast output of books, articles, speeches, and scientific discoveries that frequently astound the lay public. Moreover, the sheer appearance of knowledge and erudition, of scientific and technological complexity, serves to keep even the intelligent and educated nonspecialist from looking too closely at the institutions of academia and discovering what lies behind the public façade. The difficulty in comprehension of scientific phenomena creates the possibility of a fraud, which in view of the possibilities inherent in modern science are still not exploited to their full potential.

An amazingly large number of academicians *are* genuinely disinterested. They support the eternal verities, beauty, truth, art, culture, and liberal, humanitarian causes. In this respect they represent a reservoir of talent supporting the higher ideals and aspirations of our society. Some of these ideals and aspirations are based upon purely professional concerns; for example, a professor of painting is expected to like art. Yet many, perhaps the vast majority of professors, entered their respective fields with the realization that they could earn more in some other profession.

At the same time, the "science and knowledge explosion" has suddenly brought the marketplace into the academy. Vast opportunities now exist for the application of knowledge and techniques which previously only bestowed honorific benefits. As a result, the academicians are increasingly "interested" and concerned with "mundane," "practical," and "more lowly" affairs. Increasingly they sell themselves to the highest bidders, though it is still considered preferable to sell one-self to a government agency, a foundation, or a union than to a lowly commercial, profit-making organization. As yet, the new applied sciences have not completely penetrated the university. Some universities are "backward"; others respect their past traditions. And the full understanding of the commercial talent available in the university has not reached all would-be purchasers of such talent. The ideology of science and the disinterested search for truth remains the most important selling point for the university professor who wishes to cash in on his talents.

While recognizing all these weaknesses, we must also recognize that the university provides the possibility of a life where ideals can be advanced and where much of the best elements of our culture are carefully preserved. There are many devoted, honorable, idealistic, and truly uncorrupted men on the campus. One can only hope that the proportion of such men on the campus will not decrease in the future.

All this does not alter the fact that, in terms of personal ethics, the university all too frequently resembles a cesspool. The universities have the highest ethical standards and are among the lowest in performance of all the professions here studied. Many individuals are ethically and morally superior. But these are deviants from the operative standards of their environment. Why this is true is indeed an intriguing question. We believe that it is primarily because of personal failure that individuals become ethically and morally corroded. We have indicated that the university post offers the professor the greatest opportunities for professional and personal self-realization. All that is required for self-realization is that he do in a disciplined, organized, and creative manner the work that he trained himself for. He is given the time, the opportunity, and sufficient salary to prove to himself his capability. Failure under such conditions is corrosive, because under these conditions it is difficult to blame the external environment, the cruel Philistines, or the corrupting Maecenases for one's failure. There is no one to blame but oneself, but one cannot resist trying. The deflated narcissism, the sense of boredom, the necessity for self-vindication, all result in the creation of obstacles that would justify failure. Thus the vendetta is a major way out, as are investments of inordinate amounts of time in teaching and make-work administration. Living the role of the prophet or the perennial youth leader also serves to make life meaningful. Contract research provides opportunities to do work which is requested and defined by others. It provides an external rhythm for an intense life, while teaching or self-directed research may not.

Such forms of self-dramatism and narcissism are supported by the absence of genuine, independent criteria for the value of work done. As a result, even in comparison with the advertising man, the academic man is not subjected to external discipline or standards. The choices he makes are his own, and he has more alternatives in selecting his brand of poison than does any other professional. If he develops and lives up to his own high standards, none of the worst of academic culture need be relevant to him. If he fails, the absence of standards allows him to wallow in a wide range of behavior much of which violates his own ideological, work, or ethical standards.

THE ETHICS OF THE POVERTY OFFICIAL

THE POVERTY OFFICIAL is different from both the advertising man and the academician. He inherits the worst of both worlds. There were neither internal or external ethics in the poverty program reported. There *is* a recognition in our society that poverty is evil and that poverty based on discrimination, segregation, and exploitation is evil. But opposition to the evils does not by itself constitute the basis for ethics. For an ethical system to be operative it must include some set of self-limitations that are principled rather than expedient.

The poverty program we described knew only the limits that were imposed upon it from outside, the limits placed upon it by other people's budgets, competition, and the desire to own a jurisdictional area, a valuable property called poverty. Instead of ethics there were ideologies. Each ideology served to justify whatever program and action that the individual ideologist adhered to. But the ideologies did not serve to act as limits on action. They served only to justify claims, attacks, rights, but not a sense of responsibility to the program.

There was no ethical responsibility brought to bear in actions addressed to the "white power structure." The city and various federal departments constituted both obstacles and sources of opportunity to the program. The "power structure" had both the money and the power to grant or withhold it and to control the conditions for the expenditures of funds by the project. Project executives responded in minimal ways to the power of these "masters" but did all they could to undermine these masters when expedient. It was perfectly appropriate to mislead, deceive, flatter, and be servile to these masters when useful, and to attack, insult, and abuse them for their imputed racism when they asked embarrassing questions. The extremists in the organization tended to feel even less restraint than others in dealing with the white power structure. They regarded it as the enemy and were reasonably open in doing so.

The attitude of poverty officials toward the "community," the ghetto itself, is much more complicated. Many of the board of directors, the representatives of the community, did not live in the community. Neither did the executive directors. Both executive directors were disdainful of the "community" as being totally disorganized and lacking sufficient leadership to be called a community. However, as the project began to fight city hall, the second executive director "organized" the community as a political instrument. As a result, the term "community" began to take on a new meaning. The project spoke of "representing the community" and "expressing its needs and aspirations." The term became a master symbol in conflicts with the outside "power structure," a designation that elected officials understood in terms of votes. Of course, rival and competitive organizations also claimed to represent the community.

For political purposes it was necessary to involve and perhaps create a community, that is, a viable body of public opinion. Whether, in fact, this is what did happen is not as yet known. On specific issues there were temporary agreements among those community members who participated in public events. However, the number so involved was relatively small. But throughout the entire length of the planning and summer phases of the project, the rival groups in the community were utterly fragmented and deadlocked over basic issues. In this sense the community did not exist. Perhaps the success of the project in getting funded will create a community. Certainly the leaders of the project can speak with the authority of their budgets, and many will be forced to listen to them because of the budgets.

But the issue here is, Did the idea of a "community" set any restraints on the project or did it serve only as a propaganda device? All the ideologists defended their programs or lack of them in terms of ideas of the "community." But all attempted to impose their personal or outside organizational vision upon the community. The community was only raw material for propaganda or manipulation; and since the ideologists were concerned primarily with their own message, they did not modify their views to take into account the probable response of the community. The project-oriented professionals also attempted to manipulate the community. Since they were concerned with success, they modified their aspirations to take into account the possibility of getting sufficient support to overcome their "enemies" in and outside the community. In this sense they became responsive to the community. Whether the community ever became more than a propaganda or organizational device for the community leaders or project professionals is not known. I was never

aware of any genuine response to the community. Nevertheless, even these developments represent an improvement over
the total apathy and withdrawal into the ghetto that preceded
the project.

The internal ethics of the project, as we have indicated,
were nonexistent. Ideologies served as excuses both for non-
performance so far as work and duties were concerned and
for the frequent occurrence of behavior that in all other
organizations would be regarded as morally leprous. The
highest ideals appear to justify the shabbiest behavior both in
academia and in the ghetto, but in the ghetto the absence of
standards is more striking than the violation of standards.

The absence of ethical standards can be explained not only
by the belief in absolute ideologies but also by the growth of
vast new opportunities in comparison to past opportunities.
In this sense the great opportunities for success or failure, as
in advertising, place pressures upon individuals to operate in
ways which in other settings would be considered unethical.

The new organization in a new area, in the process of
being organized, in a short time, by an inexperienced staff,
under conditions of pressure, stress, and conflict, is not likely
to start with high ethical standards. The process of bureaucratization, with the firing of incompetents, "boat rock-
ers," and undisciplined ideologists, necessarily leads to the
creation of norms of work and ethics. In this sense, the
money invested in poverty programs may not be wasted.

THE ETHICS OF SOCIAL WORK

SOCIAL WORKERS attempt to operate within the range of external *and* internal ethics. This does not mean that there are no
violations of their ethical standards. On the contrary, we have
pointed out a great number of such violations. But the violations are viewed *as violations;* they evoke negative reactions
and serve as controls over moral leprosy.

The insistence on ethical standards comes from the fact
that most social workers take the idea of service seriously.

Moreover, their jobs force them to see what ignorance, poverty, disease, and destitution can do. They are forced to deal with social reality at its worst. As a result the easy dodges and pat solutions that serve as an escape and retreat from these realities are not readily available. Numerous professional and nonprofessional social workers do attempt to develop these forms of evasion, but the structure of their work makes this more difficult than in other occupational areas.

The word "ideology" of course must be qualified. Social workers have two types of ideology; one, an ideology of service to the client, is heir to all the ideals of Judeo-Christian philanthropy and benevolence; the other, the ideology of social work *as a profession,* rests upon claims to the peculiar professional training and qualifications to do a job that no other profession or amateur can do. In part the professional claim is a claim to monopolize jobs for those who have undergone a prescribed course of graduate training. The ideology of social service, whether it comes from social work schools or not, is reinforced by the clients, who obviously need the service. Thus welfare workers and social workers tend to identify with their clients simply because their clients are so dependent on their services. By identifying with their clients (and sometimes overidentifying with them) they come to oppose their own bureaucracies, whose rules and procedures are often designed to limit the services they can offer their clients.

Their ethical codes are geared primarily to serving the clients and are thus external in orientation. As professionals they lobby for the extension of social and psychological services for their clients. Since the needs are so great, they argue for more than an increase of the number of jobs and the size of social service budgets. They become, to some degree, a conscience for society. Some will argue for changes in the structure of society in order to modify the conditions that force their clients to seek help. But here, too, the vision of the unique individual in immediate need tends to restrict their revolutionary fervor. They find it difficult to neglect their clients while advocating overall reform of the society. Since they are forced by the structure of their jobs to live with the results of their advocacy, they are likely to be responsible in formulating the solutions they advocate. They differ from ideologists, who are free to advocate extreme and radical solutions because they know these solutions are not likely to be adopted, and if adopted would become someone else's responsibility. They are thus more "conservative" than ideologists.

Of course, those welfare and social workers who become identified primarily with their professional and occupational bureacuracy are less likely to insist on other standards than those of professional service per se. "Careerist" professionals will identify, at times, with the restrictive rules of their own bureaucracies and with the professional aspiration of their trade. In part, as must be expected, the needs of the social and welfare worker become more central than those of the client. This is the case of professionalism and careerism everywhere and is not especially true of social work. However, the increasing professionalization of social work is likely to result in an increased care for the welfare of the social workers and less care for the client.

The internal ethics of social service work are based primarily upon identification with the client against the supervisor and the social service organization. It is antibureaucratic. Thus the breaking of work rules is ethical from the point of view of the field worker if it is in the client's interest, but it is unethical from the standpoint of the organization. The result is a double set of ethical norms, one from the worker's point of view and the other from an organizational point of view. The clash between these two systems of ethics is mediated by a secret language which permits illegality without involving the supervisor in the illegality. Both the supervisor and worker are able to cooperate in order to get necessary work done without allowing their differences to prevent action. Each can preserve his primary identification and both can do their respective work. Such a system is always required when individuals who differ are forced by their work or social situation to cooperate. But this system results in a complicated pattern of double-think, which is often more desirable than the open expression of differences.

It does, however, create many surrealistic situations in which each party to a social relationship is forced to protect his enemy so that his enemy can protect him, a situation not unlike that of invoking the social contract in advertising. In the community action program, where ideological differences were "openly and honestly" expressed, the ideological conflicts that ensued resulted in organization paralysis. A feeling of responsibility, then, necessarily results in some "dishonesty." In this sense, all organizations produce a necessary minimal amount of fraud. Many, of course, go beyond the minimum.

THE BUREAUCRATIZATION OF WORK

ALL FOUR of the occupational fields we have described are at least partially bureaucratized; that is, they operate on the basis of standardized procedures which constitute part of their work norms.

However, they are bureaucratized to different degrees. The academician, as a teacher, is freed, while in the classroom, from the direct supervision of a supervisor. Since the professor is regarded as a specialist in his own field, there is little that his boss can tell him about the substance of his teaching. In his own scholarly research he is subject to no rules or regulations other than those he chooses. Contract research, of course, is subject to the rules either of research organizations or of the contractors.

Advertising agencies are bureaucratic and authoritarian in nature. Only if the agency is small or is imperfectly organized is it free from the rules of bureaucratic organization.

Most social work agencies are more or less bureaucratically organized, depending on their size, and poverty programs are not bureaucratically organized only if haste and confusion in organization have prevented them from achieving their legally defined forms.

The advertising man's response to bureaucracy is entirely different from that of professionals in these other fields. De-

spite the fact that work in an advertising agency is subject to
infinitely greater stresses, anxiety, insecurity, and pressures,
those who do not break, adjust and take pride in overcoming
the pressures. To be able to handle pressure, surmount it, is
the greatest virtue among advertising men. The capacity to
accept the heightened pressure and a bureaucratic framework
is due in part to the lack of an ideology. The advertising man
has no independent ideology which enables him to stand
apart and judge his organization. He must operate within the
framework and goals of his organization (which are not
ideologically determined) because he lacks these independent
standards. His goals become psychological and material in
nature. Strength, finesse, capacity for work and dissimulation,
control of impulse, and pride in skill, all replace the immanent values of the work. For the social worker, academician, and poverty worker there are ideologies that are independent of the organization. The disinterested pursuit of
science, knowledge, and culture, the rescuing of individuals
from the depths of misery, poverty, ignorance, and disease or
other forms of degradation, are independent of any particular
organization. The organization is only a means to achieve
these ultimate ends. Since it is only a means, it is subjected to
criticisms of even the lowliest staff members who have inde-
pendently internalized these ends. If, as in advertising, there
are no highly ideologized ultimate ends in the organization,
the individual does not have the moral and ideological basis
for criticizing or feeling superior to the organization. He is on
the same moral plane as his bosses.

As a result, in all nonprofit work areas it is extremely
difficult for the top officials to discipline, organize, and control the lower ranks. The lower ranks set up their own goals
for the organization and attempt, in violation of their bureaucratic obligations and position, to move the entire organization along a path they have predetermined. Ideologists, from
the standpoint of their bureaucratic bosses, thus become irresponsible, undisciplined, and disloyal officials. Wherever
possible, high-level bureaucrats purge the ideologists. They do
this not primarily out of ideological concerns, but only to
develop a responsive, disciplined, loyal, and technically com-

petent staff. At the same time, the bureaucratic elites will use existing ideologies relative to their field as means of advancing their respective organizations. Thus, to the bureaucratic elite, the only acceptable ideologists among their staff are those that support the organizational purposes at any given time. As a result the bureaucracy as a form attacks all independent ideologies and replaces them by forms of ideological expediency. In addition it worships competence, discipline, self-control, and self-management, technical virtuosity, nerve, and an achievement motivation that is detached from the end or the values which the organization is set up to serve.

The bureaucratic ideology tends to replace all other ideologies as bureaucratic forms of organization begin to predominate in business, government, universities, philanthropy, and other occupational areas. The bureaucratic attack on independent ideologies takes the form of not hiring ideologists, firing them, retraining personnel to accept the bureaucratic ethos, and promoting those who do. It takes the form of doing these same things at the level of graduate and undergraduate education so that, if successful, the system operates to preselect only those who can conform.

Sooner or later potential bureaucrats (bureaucratic employment is the largest source of professional and white collar work in our society) must see the light if they wish to succeed with or without trying. They are forced to make themselves over to meet the requirements for success in bureaucratic society. They have plenty of help in this re-creation.

In this sense we can talk of "the end of ideology." Bureaucracy needs very little independent ideology. As bureaucracy grows, all other forms of ideology are depressed because the occupational and economic rewards of nonideological commitment are made more attractive. The capable, competent, technically trained, disciplined, ideological, and morally neutral individual becomes the cynosure of a bureaucratic world; the other-oriented, organizational man is simply the domesticated bureaucrat.

These processes are implicit in the range of occupations previously discussed. In the community action program, a totally new area, the presence of ideology was a predominate feature, resulting in the inability of the executive directors to control their staff. After wholesale firings and forced resignations, a new breed of black bourgeois became the predominant staff official, a caricature of the bureaucrat. There is little doubt that, after the passage of time, the caricature will become the real thing. In social work and in the academic trades the conflict between ideological and organizational commitment dominates the culture of the organization. Because both sets of commitment in these fields are strong, the conflict is likely to be a lasting one. However, the tremendous resources and organizational efficiency of bureaucracy result in an ever-increasing bureaucratization of work, and the reduction or control by bureaucratic elites of its ideological content. Advertising has totally achieved this control, and as a result psychological values replace ideological ones.

BUREAUCRACY AND THE RHYTHM OF WORK

BUREAUCRATIC ORGANIZATION takes the form of a strict, mechanical delineation of tasks in an ordered sequence of operations to meet the needs of the overall operation of an organization as defined by bureaucratic or superbureaucratic elites. The individual must adjust his needs, work rhythms, and psychological states and moods to the requirements of an organization. The opposite of bureaucratic organization in this respect might be that of the painter or independent writer who can, if he is productive and prosperous (either through work or an independent income), lie fallow for extended periods and make up the time so lost in periods of intense, feverish creativity. He can work at night or at odd hours and appear to be an idle man when others are working.

The advertising man, in adjusting his work rhythm to the requirements of "senseless" work pressures, represses any personal rhythm that he may have. Regardless of any need to "lie fallow," to relax, or to take it easy, he disciplines his inner urges to the demands of the bureaucratic machine. In fact, the advertising man, after developing such discipline, is frequently unable to respond to a relaxation of work pressures. He invents pressure for himself and for others in order to allow for the release of narcissistic energy which accumulates as a result of his job.

A poverty program, at least in its early phases, is similar to advertising. Continual crises, in part self-engendered, create an emotional intensity in work. This intensity allows for dramatic victories and defeats, self-dramatization, overwork, and elation and enthusiasm in demonstrating one's mastery over crises. Poverty programs, however, because of their youth, tend to have all the crises of advertising with none of its discipline or routine.

Social work in established agencies tends to have a more stabilized routine of work whose rhythm is objective, that is, externally imposed. While most social workers are overworked, the sense of crisis is not a normal feature of work. The major problem of work rhythm for the social worker is how to "goof-off" successfully and still meet his minimal or self-imposed obligations.

This is a problem that most academicians have solved. The external work rhythm for the professor is embodied in the requirement that he meet his classes at fixed times and places for six, nine, twelve, or fifteen hours a week, that he grade exams in a predetermined time period, and that he take on a number of committee assignments. All other forms of discipline and work rhythm are determined by himself. Since the external discipline and work rhythms are so slight, the academician can, to all intents and purposes, achieve the autonomy to determine his own pace and tasks. We have indicated that the vast majority of professors fail to use this structurally determined autonomy for the purposes embodied in their obligations to their colleges, their students, or themselves. Instead they invent vastly complicated social, psychological, and organizational devices which enable them to avoid the responsibilities explicit and implicit in their positions. The vendetta, politicizing, the ritualization of teaching, "school services," and endless administration are all devices of this order, not unlike the self-engendered crises in advertising and poverty programs. Even contract research can be viewed as an attempt to submit to an external discipline and rhythm of work.

For the academician this avoidance of autonomy is particularly self-destructive. The ideology of the academic world and the personal appeal of an academic career glorify autonomous creativity and productivity. The structure of work permits it. Thus the academician who fails to use his opportunities has no one to blame but himself. And this is the most intolerable situation. For as long as he can blame the system, the bosses, the crass, vulgar public, or some other external obstacle to self-fulfillment, he can preserve his pride and sense of injured manhood despite failure to achieve his ideals. When there is no one to blame but oneself, self-hatred and despair are the likely results. It is thus not difficult to see why it is necessary to invent obstacles where none exist. Most of what we have reported of the academic scene represents the invention of obstacles, a pseudodiscipline, a pseudorhythm, and a pseudocrisis which prevent self-realization.

But such analysis does not explain why, in the light of the opportunities for creativity and productivity, so many academicians fail. It would be easy to suggest that academicians as a group are an inferior breed who develop false notions of what they can do and then find that, in reality, they are incapable of realizing these goals. There is a germ of truth in the argument. Academicians, at least in their youth, are exposed to the works of the greatest minds in the world. They identify with the beauty and clarity of thought of such men as Einstein, Freud, Keynes, Weber, Newton, and others. Among their own professors there may be several who seem to embody the quintessence of achievement. But when the academician graduates from the role of student, that is, consumer, to that of producer, he may find that it is not enough to appreciate or identify with beauty, truth, or genius. The realization may be crushing.

Another possible explanation might be that the process of graduate education rewards the insensitive, the persistent plodder, and the sycophant. As a result the successful doctoral candidate is well equipped to work under somebody else's direction, but is unequipped to be autonomous.

Both of these explanations might explain a high rate of failure, but neither explains the vast amount of time and energy used by the failures to invent objective conditions which make success impossible. Moreover, they do not account for the fact that the vast majority of academicians, whether productive or creative or not, are extremely bright and intelligent as well as energetic. Their brightness, intelligence, and energy are simply invested in self-destructive activities.

The explanation that we would choose to offer is highly speculative. We believe that each and every individual has at the biological core vast amounts of energy at his disposal, even at birth. The energy so available is more than he can channel, use, and direct, either in socially approved or in disapproved goals. The process of socialization consists in using some of the energy of the individual to block the release of other energy. Thus in developing defenses and means of repressing his own uncontrolled energy, the individual weakens the driving force that can be the source of either the greatest productivity or the greatest destructiveness in an individual. Most of the ritual, mass communications, and the ceremonies of society are devices that sponge up the energy that, if uncontrolled, might be destructive. The synthetic violence in television or in sports allows for the dissipation of aggressiveness that might without such release result in direct physical violence. Organized leisure, aggression turned against the self or dissipated in countless small feuds, serves to keep the energies of the individual from exploding in any one direction.

Occasionally the entire energy output of an individual is focused and released in one direction. At this time the individual who is so fortunate can discover that he has the strength of ten. There is no amount of work too great for him, nothing he cannot accomplish. Nothing is impossible.

An analysis of what we can call the great creative geniuses would, I am convinced, indicate that equal to their talent is the ability to organize, focus, and direct a vast amount of energy into the field that becomes the medium of their genius. Art, science, scholarship, statecraft, warfare, almost any occupational field can be the medium by which such energy is released and directed. If the individual finds such a medium and can focus all his energy in it the amount that he can accomplish is phenomenal.

The problem for our study is to account for (1) the release of energy and (2) the failure or success in finding a medium.

The release of energy is probably accounted for by a loving, warm, responsive treatment in infancy, with minimal threats, repression, and frigidity in treatment accorded the child. Warm and loving parents or parental surrogates give the infant a chance to develop psychological strength through identification. At later dates (from a year on) the parental figures must repress and inhibit the child if he is to become human. The repression simply means that he is forced to control his own behavior, appetites, and demands, and to mold them into styles and forms which evoke parental approval or at least avoid disapproval. Overrepression can result in guilt, inability to express one's primal energy, or hostility against the parent even at the expense of achieving one's own goals. Overrepression can result in overconformity. If the repression is mild and given in a loving context, the child will still resent the parent's attempts to deny him his own instinctual needs. The child will reject, in part, the world as presented by the parent and create his own imaginary, private world, one which is partially antiparental and more comfortable than that which he is being forced into. When this process takes an extreme form, the child-created world may replace the world he lives in; that is, he may become psychotic. In the normal process, this secondary world is a world of imagination, of creativity, or art and fancy. It is a world which allows the child to express his own unique image of the world and to create and re-create it along lines that give him aesthetic satisfaction. If the "demands" of reality are too strong, the child will neglect this secondary world and comfort himself with "ordinary" problems in ordinary terms. To do so he must repress even a mild phantasy world, thereby using up a substantial amount of energy necessary for such repression and control. Remaining in the here-and-now is as costly as departing from it.

If the child discovers by accident, an aspect of the "real world" that corresponds to his secondary phantasy world and he is encouraged to expand, discipline, and stylize his phantasies, the original energy invested in rebellion becomes a source of creativity. The child links the medium of literature, art, music, science, or the accumulation of knowledge to his fundamental sources of energy. The phantasy becomes a form of reality that projects the individual into the world instead of, as in the case of a psychosis, isolating him from it. This discovery of a link between one's private form of rebellion and a positive medium of culture is usually accomplished by the availability of a parent or adult figure who embodies, exemplifies, and encourages development into the field which previously had been, to him, only a phantasy. The uncle, a parent, a teacher who exemplifies the field reinforces the individual in developing systematic, stylized, and technically realized forms of his original vision. If the ideal does not become repressive and if the parental figure does not smother the child with overagreement and thereby steal the private world from the child, the parental figure confirms the child's development in an autonomous direction. When vast amounts of energy are invested in the medium, vast amounts of accomplishment are possible. If the child can transcend each parental model made available to him and can replace him with more able ones, he is capable of almost unlimited growth. Obstacles, if they are not insuperably repressive, may harden the determination of the individual as he moves onward. The threat of the withdrawal of love and affection by parents who do not approve of a child's drive to goals that do not appear to be practical can be dangerous, almost as dangerous as parental approval that is exploitative in nature. Appreciation of a child for "childish enthusiasm" followed by disapproval of the child for the same activities at a latter age because they are "childish" is likely to result in an attitude of conformance, of looking to others for goals, discipline, and work rhythms. Allowing the child to develop his own goals, discipline, and approval while providing noninterfering and nonexploitative love is a most difficult task for a parent. It requires maturity, confidence, and health, all scarce products in any society.

If all these factors are operative, the child has a chance. As he develops his own talents, he may discover that the only models he needs are those provided by his own inner demons. He can pursue them without dependence upon others. If he does so, he has at his disposal unlimited energy, a set of goals, a medium by which he expresses them, and the skill and technique to express them.

Quite frequently only a part of the process is achieved. The child or young man is able to release his energy without developing the medium for disciplining the energy so released. If this happens at a very early age, before the child learns any social controls, he may become a monster, a psychopath. All the energies of a near genius can be used to gratify purely hedonistic, antisocial needs. The individual becomes a menace who may well end up with his name in the papers. If the explosion occurs after the basic socialization of the child has been achieved, the child will look for modes of activity in the "real world" which allow him to express his energy. Unrepressed energy is a source of danger to its bearer, since it leaves him with turbulent, unsettled, and unrelieved feelings of internal pressure unless he moves, works, acts, or plays. The organized life of a society allows the individual to use its patterns of organization as a medium for releasing this energy. If the work or social organization permits only a slow, even unhurried pace, the energized individual may become a disruptive force, upsetting the pace of others in order to live by his own internal rhythm. If he can control himself, however, he can become a dynamic mover in such an organization. He can use his energy to become a pyramid climber. As such, he may be a constructive force. He may, however, be fortunate enough to find another organization whose demands upon him are such that his total energy can be absorbed by the external demands of the organization. If he is so fortunate, one can be sure that others who are either autonomous or whose rate of energy release is lower than his may be out of phase with the external rhythm and discipline of the organization.

Advertising thus allows for, in fact requires, the release of high volumes of energy by individuals who will submit to the demands of the agency in releasing their energy as required. An ideology also allows for the release of vast amounts of energy in the name of a cause or the organization that embodies the cause. It allows for the release of energy by those who find no other way in a society for expressing directly or truly energy that is hard to contain.

The academic environment is based upon the assumption that individuals have at their disposal vast amounts of energy; that their chosen field is its medium; and that they have developed the discipline, autonomy, and technique to direct it in their own work.

The failure of the vast majority of academicians to achieve the promise of their field undoubtedly rests upon the partial achievement of autonomy. The majority of academics, through a favorable social environment, have achieved the ability to release vast amounts of energy; they have acquired the techniques and the media of their respective fields. What they lack is the ability to define their own problems or the ability to discipline themselves to an autonomous work rhythm that would result in fulfilling their occupationally defined tasks. Failure to achieve this form of autonomy is destructive since the energy to do so has been released but, owing to the lack of an operative medium, has no constructive way of being expressed. All the forms of compensatory or substitute behavior are attempts to discharge this energy without directing it into the medium for which it was originally released.

In such situations, having the energy available may well be worse than not having contained the energy at a more primary or elementary level. For without a disciplined medium for being autonomous, the energy shakes, rocks, and rattles the individual. At times even the greatest discipline will not control the released energy. Van Gogh, Modigliani, Toulouse-Lautrec, Gauguin, Berlioz, Wagner, Balzac, Jack London—all are examples of an individual whose undoubted genius could not contain his energy. Cézanne, Freud, Haydn, Einstein, Henry James, and J. S. Bach are individuals who achieved some serenity despite a vast amount of energy. Others—Hugo Wolf, Beethoven, and William James, for example —alternated between fits of tormented depression and constriction and the periodic release of vast energy.

In part, such risks are necessary to the freeing of vast amounts of energy; for if the inspiration, health, or discipline fails to go with the energy, depression and withdrawal can result.

The academic world produces, perhaps at lower levels of genius, sufficient numbers of individuals who achieve some level of serenity. It produces also anguished creative individuals who are tormented either by periods of depression, fallowness, and sterility or by an excess of energy. But it produces most of all, individuals who have everything but the self-discipline and autonomy necessary for them to live with either themselves or their occupational responsibilities. Advertising achieves perhaps a better blend between occupational demands and psychological response. It does so by eliminating those who do not "fit." In the university those who do not fit are the vast majority.

THE SENSELESSNESS OF WORK

THE FUNDAMENTAL PHILOSOPHIC PROBLEM in the history of all society is how to deal with the "senselessness" of the world. The world is experienced as senseless because history, nature, and man's experience contradict all his theories and preconceptions. "The best laid schemes o' mice and men/Gang aft a-gley." War, death, revolution, disease, misfortune, strike with little relationship to the worthiness of those so afflicted, and good fortune often falls to those who are deemed to be unworthy.

In some way, all individuals at all times suffer from the experience of the senselessness of the world. They attempt either to understand the world, to render it "meaningful" by developing a theory that explains its "senselessness," or to control the world or one another by science or magic. So far we have failed in these attempts. The more professional and complicated our theories become, the more they are removed from the ordinary experience we wish them to explain. Moreover, we are increasingly able to develop the critical abilities to discover the fallacies in our own theories. Finally, so far, science has not enabled us to deal with the irrationality of war and total destruction; and taking the world as a whole, the problems of poverty, misery, disease, and starvation are multiplying faster than the solutions. One might argue that man as an experiment is a failure.

Each of the various occupational fields confronts the problem of senselessness in its own way.

The social worker attempts to repair the damage by providing services to his clients. He most often feels he is bailing out a leaky boat with a sieve. Despite this, he attempts to help in his own way, realizing that at best he will help repair some damage after it has occurred, while still more damage is being done. The ideologist attempts to make the world "sensible" by remaking it. He must avoid facing the fact that, all too frequently, while he opposes the bureaucratization of present society, he will, if successful, be the advance agent for even more destructive forms of bureaucratization of society. In the meantime, he is likely to be destructive in his occupational world, if only to prove his own sincerity and commitment to higher values.

The academician as social philosopher and humanist attempts to understand the world, and the scientist attempts to help control it. He does not know who will yield this control or for what purposes. In the meantime many sell their services to the highest bidder; and most, despite their high ideals, either "goof-off" or create a personal and institutional culture which gives the lie to their aspirations.

The advertising man confronts the senselessness of the world in a unique and modern way. Instead of talking about it or attempting to correct it, he lives it. Mastering the senselessness of the world by living it, results in an ethic of self-mastery, pride, and a definition of virtues that makes personal survival in a senseless world the greatest of all virtues. The Philistine (in our age the bureaucrat) who accepts, without questioning, the opportunities inherent in any given situation is equally a modern man, adjusted to whatever form modern society takes. But Philistines have always existed: only the form changes, with the passage of time.

Beyond this, the continuous attempt to pierce the "senselessness of the world," even if unsuccessful, results in the most sublime works of art, literature, music, science, philosophy, and the social sciences. The creation and enjoyment of these modes of science, knowledge, and sensibility represent the highest achievements of man. As long as man continues to attempt to solve the puzzle of the senselessness of the world, his experiment cannot be judged a failure. Failure consists only in surrender.